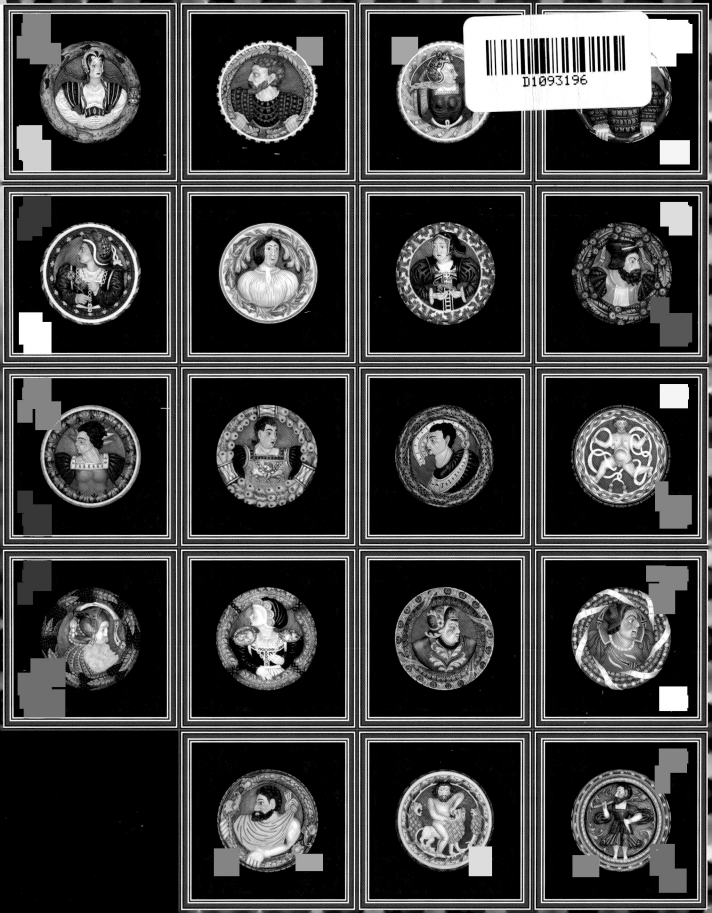

REBIRTH OF A PALACE

The Royal Court at Stirling Castle

First published by Historic Scotland 2011
Printed from sustainable materials 2011
© Crown copyright 2011

British Library Cataloguing-in-Publication Data. A CIP catalogue record for
this book is available from the British Library.

ISBN 978-1-84917-055-0

REBIRTH OF A PALACE

The Royal Court at Stirling Castle

John G. Harrison

CONTENTS

Foreword   10

1 The Scottish Court   13
   A theatrical setting for royal life

2 The Stirling Castle Palace Project   27
   Re-creating magnificence

3 The Architecture, Statues and Sculpture   39
   Structures and symbolism

4 Furnishings, Walls and Fittings   61
   Formality and function

5 Costume and Jewellery   83
   A courtly dress code

6 The Unicorn Tapestries   105
   Weaving stories

7 The Stirling Heads   131
   Portraits in oak

   Epilogue   162

   Further Reading, Credits and Acknowledgements   164

FOREWORD

by Fiona Watson

Stirling Castle cannot help but impose. From whatever angle you approach, it sits triumphantly on its craggy perch above the floodplain of the River Forth, emerging ethereally out of the early morning mist or catching the sun's rays on the golden walls of the Great Hall. Controlling the Forth crossing between north and south, the castle naturally made a statement about the power of those in charge of such a strategically-important place. And thus it is no accident that some of the most momentous and bloody events in Scotland's history have taken place within sight of these walls.

But let us imagine that we are friend, not foe. The year is 1549. Seven years ago, King James V died suddenly in his prime, leaving a week-old baby girl as his successor. But the kingdom survived, the Stewart dynasty is secure – thanks in part to the astuteness of James's widow, the Frenchwoman, Mary of Guise. Even the ambitious building project that James had planned for Stirling has been brought to fruition.

Those who passed through the splendidly turreted gatehouse would naturally have glanced up to the left at the new Palace, at the cornucopia of statues girding its exterior, extolling the need for warlike vigilance, the virtues of good government and its reward of peace and plenty – Renaissance themes interpreted for a Scottish palate. Tonight lights flicker through the windows – the Queen Mother is in residence. A handful of invited guests – a favoured Scottish earl and his wife, perhaps, or the French ambassador – push their way through the servants and hangers-on in the Queen's Outer Hall,

smoothing down gowns and doublets, checking hats and headdresses. Most visitors never make it past this point and, whatever their purpose, would be made to wait long enough to admire the room's many enchanting features. Mary often dines here, but tonight her special guests pass on.

And here they might well pause. The Queen's Inner Hall is truly splendid, deep red walls covered in a gold floral motif, painted to part like curtains around the doors and fireplace. The wooden panels in the ceiling are decorated in black, cream and white, intricate motifs framing portraits of James and Mary. Most sumptuous of all are the seven tapestries surmounting the walls: exquisite, vastly expensive and laden with symbolism. The Queen Mother wishes no one to doubt the antiquity and nobility of the two lines that combined to produce the current Queen of Scots and the future Queen of France, her daughter, Mary.

A door in the opposite wall opens and peals of laughter break through. The visitors hurry on, into the Queen Mother's own Bedchamber, the tasteful green of the paintwork vying with rich damask wall hangings. Here symbolism and display are still paramount – personal objects and comfortable living arrangements are confined to Closets out of bounds to all but an intimate few. But there is still much amusement to be had – witty, well-educated talk, music, perhaps, even some dancing and a little buffoonery. Mary of Guise knows how to entertain, how to enlighten and engage, at the same time advancing her own position at the heart of Scottish politics.

In taking the bold step to re-create Stirling's Royal Lodgings in their full 16th-century glory, Historic Scotland has given us all access to the everyday lives of extraordinary people. It is *an* interpretation of course, a well-researched conjecture as to what was once here. The décor, the fittings and furnishings, the costumes and, of course, the years of painstaking research and superb workmanship that underpin this incredible enterprise allow us not only to walk through the deliberately glorious apartments of one of the most enduring and successful dynasties of medieval and early modern Europe. We can also, if we look hard enough, catch a glimpse of the men and women who once lived here, those who visited, and the scores of craftsmen, attendants and servants who kept the whole show on the road – whether that is in the faces of the famous Stirling Heads, recast in glorious colour and detail to adorn the King's Inner Hall, or in the swish of a sumptuous gown worn by a costumed interpreter.

This is a jewel beyond compare, to amaze us all today and for many years, perhaps centuries, to come, just as James and Mary intended. I very much hope that you enjoy this beautiful book, which reveals a lot more about the painstaking research and the intricate craftsmanship that lies behind the re-presented Royal Lodgings.

Fiona Watson is an historian, author and broadcaster based near Stirling. A former senior lecturer in history at the University of Stirling, she fronted a ten-part BBC television history of Scotland in 2001 and has made numerous radio programmes, including a series on The Enlightenment and another using original sources to highlight the experience of war across the ages entitled *Voices from the Front*. She is currently a presenter of *Making History* on BBC Radio 4. Her books include *Under the Hammer: Edward I and Scotland, 1286–1307* (1997), *Scotland: A History 8000 BC–AD 2000* (2001) and *Macbeth: A True Story* (2010).

1 THE SCOTTISH COURT
A THEATRICAL SETTING FOR ROYAL LIFE

The palace within Stirling Castle is the best-preserved 16th-century royal residence in Britain. In its heyday, it was a place of astonishing grandeur and sophistication. This book tells the story of what it was like and how it fell into a decline lasting almost 400 years. It also describes how the interiors have been re-created, allowing visitors to experience the overwhelming magnificence of the original decorative scheme.

The Palace was built for King James V, who used Stirling's stunning and historic setting to create one of Scotland's most impressive buildings and one of Britain's finest Renaissance palaces. The Stirling Castle Palace Project, which rediscovered and revived the Palace's lost glories, lasted almost ten years and was completed in 2011. It involved major research programmes, which have not only greatly enlarged our knowledge of the building itself, but have also enriched our understanding of Scotland's past – and the nation's place within European culture. The project also deployed a wide range of artists and craftspeople and so has served to foster the skills of the past.

Left: Stirling Castle seen from the north-west. The Great Hall is at the left, while the magnificent Palace is just visible at the top right, its roof topped by a carved stone lion.

A ROYAL RESIDENCE

Wealthy and powerful people have always sought to impress others by the magnificence of their residences. That sort of display has rarely been used to more effect than by the elites of 16th-century Europe. Rich colours and luxurious fabrics, gold and silver objects were not only used to impress; they also provided the stage upon which the glittering court could act out the drama of royal life. The entire Palace at Stirling was designed to convey messages about the ruling dynasty and national identity while proclaiming the wisdom, learning and piety of the monarch who commissioned it.

The Royal Lodgings provided a setting for formal rituals, such as the reception of ambassadors. They also served very practical functions ranging from the security of the royal family to the service of meals, and the provision of toilet facilities. This was, indeed, a palace for a king – though James V's death in 1542, at the age of only 30, meant that he perhaps never saw it finished. It became the childhood home of his heir and daughter, Mary Queen of Scots, and the setting for some dramatic events during her difficult and turbulent reign.

Above: The Great Hall, built by James IV around 1503, the grandest building of its kind in Scotland, and a precursor of the magnificent Palace begun 35 years later.

Above: A late-medieval banquet scene from *The Very Rich Hours of the Duke of Berry*, a French manuscript of the 1400s, provides a glimpse of the tradition of conspicuous wealth and flamboyant design inherited by Renaissance monarchs.

Stirling Castle had been a royal residence since at least the early 1100s – and, in the 1500s, myths of a Roman origin and association with King Arthur added to its prestige. From about 1490, James IV had begun to transform Stirling Castle into a thoroughly modern residence. He built the King's Old Building and the Great Hall, while also creating a grand Forework with gateway and towers. He reorganised the Chapel Royal within the castle, providing it with new revenues for an enlarged staff, making it the main focus of his formal religious life (this building has now gone, though a new Chapel Royal was commissioned by James VI in 1594).

James IV revitalised the gardens and parks, to provide walks and vistas, as well as hunting and sporting facilities, right on the castle's doorstep. And it was during his reign that work began on building the east end of Stirling's Church of the Holy Rude, just below the castle. Perhaps he also began work on the Palace, re-aligning the main buildings within the castle to form ranges on the four sides of a courtyard – an arrangement typical of the Renaissance era. Such radical and extensive work implies a serious attempt to enhance the castle's status and to give it a more significant role. But any such plans ended with his untimely death at the Battle of Flodden in 1513. The son who succeeded him as James V was barely a year old.

Top: James IV, who began Stirling's transformation into a Renaissance residence.

Above: The Forework, added by James IV, as it may have looked on completion around 1500. It survives, but has been much reduced.

AN AMBITIOUS YOUNG KING

By the late 1530s, James V resumed work at Stirling, incorporating existing buildings into his new Palace. In 1536 he set off for an extended visit to France, where he travelled extensively, spending time as a guest of King Francis I and above all looking for a bride. On 1 January 1537, he married Francis's daughter Madeleine de Valois at Notre Dame Cathedral in Paris. This was a major diplomatic coup for the king of a small country. His marriage also brought him a very substantial dowry. But when the frail Madeleine died within a few weeks of arriving in Scotland, Francis sponsored a second marriage, this time to Mary of Guise. This intelligent woman, whose family were major French nobles, brought James another hefty dowry.

So, James V could afford to build, and to build lavishly. He would create a new residence for himself and his bride, one which was truly fitting, with furnishings and decorations of a magnificence hitherto unseen in Scotland. Indeed, the marriage contract obliged him to fit Stirling out in the most fashionable style, as it was to be the dower house for Mary of Guise – the place where she would live in the event of his death.

The Royal Lodgings provided stately accommodation and reception rooms for the king and the queen, but they did not function alone. Above were rooms for courtiers and attendants. There was storage space on the floor below. The west wing, with its gallery looking out over the park, was a very fashionable attribute (though it would collapse by the early 1620s). Beneath it were the king's and queen's kitchens.

Above: Madeleine de Valois, the frail first wife of James V.

Above: James V and his second wife, Mary of Guise. As in the Stirling Head representing Mary, she holds a flower in her right hand, identifying her as a bride.

Above: The arms of Madeleine de Valois and Mary of Guise, presented side by side in a 16th-century book of heraldry.

Elsewhere within the castle, there was more accommodation for the household and for administration, while the Great Kitchen could cater for hundreds of people. The Great Hall not only provided space for major entertainments and feasts but was also where the lower tiers of the household routinely ate. Outside the castle, there were laundry facilities and stables in addition to the extensive gardens and park, while the town provided supplementary accommodation and supplies. So, the castle and its environs did not just provide the royal residence but all the support services a monarch needed.

These extensive facilities demanded extensive staff. Those attending on the king and queen included people with very practical duties (such as stable staff and cooks) and others with more ceremonial duties, often nobles and sometimes clergy. The royal court was not a specific place, but an inner core of senior members of the royal family, along with their attendants. When the king or queen moved, the court moved too.

As at most of the other royal residences, there were two royal suites: the king's and the queen's. This was necessary since both had their own staff (and even their own kitchens) and they could lead surprisingly separate and independent lives. Of course, when both were resident together, they and their households would meet, with shared use of facilities, entertainments and so on. But if only one of the royal couple was present, only the suite in current use would be fully furnished and equipped. Valuable hangings and even furniture were regularly moved between the residences.

Above: Kitchen staff at work in a 16th-century Italian painting. It is likely that similar scenes would have been witnessed in the kitchens at Stirling Castle.

AN OPEN DOOR?

There is a simple logic to the layout of the royal suites. The rooms lead one from another as was usual in grand residences of the 1500s. There is no corridor, so it is necessary to go through the outer rooms to access the inner, more private ones. Doors were usually installed against walls but, in the Queen's Inner Hall, they are in diagonally opposite corners. This is partly because the Inner Hall and Bedchamber incorporate parts of older buildings, and pre-existing fires and flues influenced the layout. But it also meant that, when the queen emerged from her Bedchamber and the crowd in the room fell back to allow her progress, more people lined the royal route.

Though there were ushers to watch the doors, there was probably a rule of thumb that, if the door ahead was open, you could pass on to the next room; if it was closed, you had reached the limits of your welcome.

One door was of pivotal importance: the one between the King's and Queen's Bedchambers. The Palace Project has revealed a fascinating fact about this door: it opened into the Queen's Bedchamber not the King's, and this means that it could only be locked and unlocked from her side, rather than his!

Above: A petitioner's-eye view of the Queen's Inner Hall, from the doorway of the Queen's Outer Hall, with the Queen's Bedchamber beyond. The arrangement of doorways meant that the queen would progress diagonally through the room, allowing more courtiers to greet her.

1 King's Outer Hall
2 King's Inner Hall
3 King's Bedchamber
4 King's Closets
5 Queen's Outer Hall
6 Queen's Inner Hall
7 Queen's Bedchamber
8 Lion's Den

Above: A cutaway illustration of the Palace, showing the arrangement of the King's and Queen's Lodgings.

THE JESTER – A COURTLY CLOWN

This is one of the Stirling Heads – the carved wooden roundels which now, once again, decorate the ceiling of the King's Inner Hall. Everyone will recognise this figure as the court jester. Jesters were just one of the many and diverse forms of entertainment available at Stirling, which ranged from hunting to reading, from sports to music, from chess to witty conversation.

But like so many of the Heads, the jester is enigmatic, provoking many questions and providing few answers. Is this a portrait of one of the real jesters or just intended to give a general impression? Has he just told a good joke? Or is he laughing at the folly of it all, the expensive, glittering pretence that kings and queens are better than fools? Should we laugh with him? Or is he laughing at us?

This roundel is identified as number 36 of the 38 oak carvings known to have survived. The numbering system is drawn from an account of the Heads published in 1960 by the Royal Commission on the Ancient and Historical Monuments of Scotland.

Two further Heads were destroyed in a fire in 1940; however replicas have been made from surviving illustrations. These have been numbered 39 and 40. Finally, there is a new 'replica' Head (see page 143), numbered 41.

A COURT ON THE MOVE

The frequent moves (which might involve several hundred people) were an essential part of the Scots royal lifestyle. They displayed royal authority around the country. They might also include breaks for hunting or other leisure activities. When the court was elsewhere, the residences could be cleaned and repaired. With four main residences – at Stirling, Holyrood, Linlithgow and Falkland – and over 20 minor ones, there was plenty of choice. Nor did this exhaust the options, for kings and queens frequently stayed in monasteries or in the houses of the nobility. A visit to Stirling might be very brief – time for something to eat and then move on. Or it might last weeks or even months. In between, the small resident staff might put fabrics and hangings into storage, and the whole place would be very quiet.

Above: Falkland Palace in Fife, the most rural of Scotland's main royal palaces.

ACCESS TO THE PALACE

At Stirling, visitors entered the Palace from the Inner Close. The unheated transe or corridor here was patrolled by lowly members of the hall staff, whose tasks included keeping out the many humble people who could easily access the outer parts of the castle. The visitor who got past the transe would then enter the Outer Hall of the king's or queen's suite. Here he might find the guard – though at one stage James V's guard consisted of only one crossbowman! He would also find people waiting to be admitted, or to catch the royal eye when the king or queen came out. It was probably in their Outer Halls that the king and queen ate many of their meals, with their guests ranged in order of precedence, down a long table. When the evening meal was over and the trestle tables cleared away, these big rooms provided ample space for courtly entertainment such as music and dancing.

The door to the next room was watched by the ushers of the outer door. Senior nobles could pass into the Inner Hall more or less on demand, but others could be turned away. The Inner Hall might be used for council meetings and for some of the more formal meals. But this was also where you were most likely to see that classic courtly scene: the splendidly-dressed king or queen, sitting on a chair of state on a raised dais, under a canopy of estate, to receive the formal visits of ambassadors, courtiers or nobles. Now a riot of colour, of rich fabrics and complex patterns, the Queen's Inner Hall in particular shows just what 16th-century magnificence was like.

Substantial crowds could assemble in the Inner Hall if the king or queen was within the inner part of the suite. People in the Inner Hall were regulated by the ushers of the inner door, who held a higher rank than the ushers of the outer door, with greater authority over this more prestigious crowd. And beyond them lay the Bedchambers, where the king and queen spent much of their time. Admission here was a privilege, though senior nobles might be annoyed if refused access too often. Perhaps neither king nor queen actually slept in the great formal beds in their Bedchambers – indeed, they probably slept somewhere else altogether. But, when she felt unwell, Mary Queen of Scots sometimes received ambassadors while sitting up in bed – perhaps a message of trust and intimacy to the monarchs whom they represented, rather than a personal privilege for the ambassadors.

Above: The King's Outer Hall, a waiting and reception area sometimes used for meals and entertainments.

Above: The Queen's Outer Hall, the equivalent room in the Queen's Lodgings.

Above: The Queen's Inner Hall, used for audiences with the monarch.

Above The King's Bedchamber, a more private space used for confidential meetings, but not usually for sleeping.

HERALDRY: ROMILLY SQUIRE

Heraldry was important to the royalty and aristocracy of the 1500s. Displaying coats of arms associated the owner with the chivalric past and could also make specific claims about ancestry and status.

Heraldry is a significant part of the Palace decoration – on fabrics, fireplaces, walls and glass. But Romilly Squire, who advised on heraldic design at Stirling, believes most contemporaries knew little about heraldry. 'Families changed their arms over the generations or even over their own lifetimes,' he says, 'and just like today, many probably had not a clue about heraldry. The artists didn't understand it either, so coats of arms were often badly drawn.'

The royal arms of Scotland bear a lion rampant (reared up on its hind legs). The supporters, standing to either side, are unicorns. The crown above indicates, by its form, that these are the arms of an independent king.

As queen of Scotland, Mary of Guise combined her own family arms with those of Scotland. The arms of a married couple are traditionally shown impaled (side by side). The husband's arms are on the dexter side – the right from the point of view of the person holding the shield – with the wife's on the sinister (left) side. The lozenge on Mary's Bedchamber ceiling is based on a heraldic illustration produced in the 1500s for Sir David Lyndsay, the Lord Lyon – Scotland's official regulator of heraldry.

Mary's arms proclaim her descent from the powerful French house of Lorraine. They include three birds, sometimes shown pierced by a single arrow – a feat allegedly achieved by her ancestor Godefroy de Bouillon, a crusader knight and one of the Nine Worthies (see page 140). They also include a Jerusalem cross, indicating ancestral claims to the throne of Jerusalem. Other motifs assert claims to European territories. Such display presented her as a woman of illustrious descent.

The arms on Mary's cloths of estate (suspended behind her chairs of state) are drawn from a portrait, though Romilly emphasises that this form is rare in Scotland. All heraldic displays throughout the Palace have been approved by the present Lord Lyon.

Above: Romilly Squire working with heraldic records.

Above (left to right): The royal arms with unicorn supporters in the King's Outer Hall; the arms of Mary of Guise as queen of Scotland on the ceiling of the Queen's Bedchamber.

THE MOST PRIVATE CHAMBERS

Beyond the Bedchambers were the Closets, sometimes also called Cabinets. These Closets were used to store things, perhaps for private 'office work' or for prayer or study. They would also have held a 'stool of ease' (toilet facilities). At Stirling, the Queen's Closets were three small linked rooms, off the Bedchamber, giving access to a private terrace walk and perhaps, also, a way out to the Outer Close. Demolished in the 1700s, they are the one part of the former lodgings which has totally vanished. The Closets were essentially private spaces, accessed only by the monarch or their personal attendants, so perhaps, in these rather cramped spaces, there was more of an eye to comfort than to display. But when Mary Queen of Scots was presented with a portrait of the King of Denmark she told the ambassador she would put it in her Cabinet. She wanted to indicate that he was close to her diplomatically, just as she once ostentatiously put a letter from Elizabeth I of England into her bosom, next to her skin, a gesture which she knew the ambassador would report.

AN INNOVATIVE DESIGN SCHEME

The style and detail of the Palace interiors were radically new and fashionable. James V was telling the world that he understood what being a Renaissance king on a European model was about. Even if he had not encountered these new styles of decoration on his trip to France, there were plenty of Scots who had wide experience of Europe. Foreigners of many countries visited Scotland too, and new ideas now circulated faster than ever before, thanks to the availability of printed books. But the layout was relatively conservative, retaining a Scots tradition of ready access to the monarch. For the tiers of exclusion which surrounded Scots kings were as nothing compared to those surrounding many others. The English court was particularly 'exclusive'; many closed doors isolated Henry VIII within his residences, an architecture which signified the retreat of the monarch from the public eye – and from the public ear. The architecture of Scottish royal residences, on the contrary, signified that, however splendid the setting, the monarch remained accessible; he could be seen and he was listening. It was a metaphor for the idealised relationship of monarch and nation.

Left: The devotional triptych created for the Queen's Bedchamber. The prayer table would more likely have stood in the queen's private Closets.

Above left: King Henry VIII of England.

Above right: Henry eating alone in his privy chamber, an inner, private space.

We can see this comparative intimacy most vividly in the Scots royal dining protocol. For, while many other monarchs routinely ate in private within the inner recesses of their suites, Scots monarchs often dined in the outer parts and with substantial and diverse company. While they ate, they participated in the general conversation – and we can imagine that an invitation was a considerable honour. The best-recorded detail is for Mary of Guise in 1549, when she never dined alone but shared her table with men and women, with Scots and French, with nobles and commoners, with bishops and ambassadors as well as quite modest army officers. No wonder she was regarded as accessible and well-informed.

Still, if James V or Mary Queen of Scots wanted to avoid the pressures of business and the stress of the public gaze, they could easily move to one of their other, more private residences such as rural Falkland.

So, at Stirling James planned the ideal residence to live out the royal dream, and work was under way by about May 1538. Only Stirling could provide such an aura of antiquity allied to practical modernity, and a satisfactory compromise between privacy and access. It was far enough from Edinburgh to be able to exclude business but not so far as to be out of touch.

But the years that followed proved traumatic. In April 1541, the royal couple's two infant sons died within days of each other. By early summer 1542, hopes for an heir were rising again, as the queen was pregnant. But summer and autumn saw a resurgence of war with England, ending with the defeat of the Scots army at Solway Moss. The baby was born at Linlithgow in early December. It was a girl – and her birth was followed almost immediately by the death of the king. And so, Mary Queen of Scots inherited the throne in troubled times, just one week old.

Above: An informal meal in the Queen's Outer Hall. Although her courtiers remain at a respectful distance, Mary of Guise enjoys convivial conversation with them.

THE INFANT QUEEN

Mary of Guise spent the next few months at Linlithgow with the little queen. A move to Stirling was probably always her aim; it was stronger than Linlithgow, further from the Border where there was a risk of the little queen being kidnapped by the English. Mary of Guise could insist on her own rights under the marriage contract. In July 1543 she and her daughter made the move. It was at Stirling that Mary Queen of Scots was crowned and this remained their main home until summer 1548, when the child queen was sent to continue her education at the French court. Mary of Guise lived mainly in Edinburgh thereafter, though her visits remained regular and several times she spent Christmas at Stirling.

Following the death of James V, James Hamilton, 2nd Earl of Arran, was appointed regent on behalf of the infant queen. He was her distant kinsman and would have inherited the throne himself if she had died. Arran resigned in favour of Mary of Guise in 1554 – a transfer of power for which he was rewarded with the wealthy French dukedom of Châtelherault. Mary of Guise then governed Scotland as regent until her own death in June 1560.

She proved a stout defender of her daughter's interests; she was skilled at placating wounded pride and at uniting conflicting groups of Scots. She achieved two major diplomatic coups. First, she secured French support for Scotland against the 'Rough Wooings'. This was a series of English attacks aimed at forcing the Scots to accept a marriage between Mary Queen of Scots and Edward, son and heir of Henry VIII. Second, and as the price of that support, she was instrumental in getting agreement for the eventual marriage of Mary to Francis, the heir to the throne of France. That marriage finally took place in 1558, when Mary was 15 and Francis only 14. On the death of his father in 1559 they became king and queen of France until the following year when Francis died, setting the stage for Mary's return to Scotland.

The Stirling Castle Palace Project has recreated the interiors of the best-preserved royal suite of the period surviving in Britain, as they might have been during Mary's childhood. But that is just the final phase of a much longer project at Stirling, involving the conservation, presentation and restoration of the Great Kitchens, the Great Hall and James VI's Chapel Royal. Substantial parts of the defences also survive, with important parts of the surrounding landscapes, including remains of the gardens and the park. So, Stirling now presents a unique opportunity to see not just the domestic setting of 16th-century royal life, but something of the wider context, too.

Above left: James Hamilton, 2nd Earl of Arran, who governed Scotland as regent from the death of James V in 1542 until his resignation in favour of Mary of Guise in 1554.

Above right: A double portrait of Francis II and Mary Queen of Scots during their brief life together as king and queen of France.

MARY QUEEN OF SCOTS AND HER SUITORS

The accession of Mary to the throne of Scotland was of European importance. Whoever married her would become king of this small but strategically important country.

If Mary died, she would be succeeded by her distant cousin, James Hamilton, Earl of Arran, who was 'but a heartbeat from the throne'. Mary's marriage to his son would unite the Hamilton and Stewart claims, but would be bitterly resented by the Hamiltons' enemies and might risk civil war.

English policy was for a marriage between Mary and Edward, young son of Henry VIII, so uniting the two kingdoms. That would secure England's northern frontier and greatly strengthen its hand against other European powers, particularly France.

France, on the contrary, wanted Scots support against England and was willing to offer a marriage to secure it. A French marriage would thwart Henry VIII's plans just as an English marriage would thwart France. And since Mary was a great-granddaughter of Henry VII of England, she was next in line after Henry VIII and his heirs. Indeed, a generation later, Mary's son James would inherit the English throne, on the death of Henry VIII's daughter Elizabeth I.

So, in the early 1540s, Scotland held a card of European importance. It was a card to play with care. A favoured strategy for the first few years was to promise much and deliver little. But England's strategy of repeated attacks and occupation of parts of Scotland (the 'Rough Wooings') proved counterproductive. In 1548 the Scots agreed to Mary's going to France and her eventual marriage to Francis, the dauphin.

Above (clockwise from top): Mary Queen of Scots at the age of nine; the dauphin Francis; Prince Edward of England; and a later portrait of James Hamilton, son of the 2nd Earl of Arran.

2 THE STIRLING CASTLE PALACE PROJECT
RE-CREATING MAGNIFICENCE

It is a strange irony that the briefness of the Palace's life
as a major royal residence probably led to its survival.
In 1603, James VI of Scotland inherited the English throne
and went south for his coronation as James I of England.
He returned only once to his homeland, in 1617,
and Scotland's royal palaces were virtually abandoned.
Stirling Palace, completed barely 60 years earlier, had lost
the main reason for its existence. But it survived and now,
for the first time in 400 years, visitors can view these
splendid spaces as they were meant to be seen.

If James and his successors had remained in Scotland, this story could have been very different.
Interiors of the 1500s were very vulnerable to poor maintenance and even more vulnerable to
changing fashions – which is why surviving examples are so rare. Perhaps, for a century or so,
it would have been possible to redecorate and make the basic structure serve changing needs.
But the day would have come when alterations were made to create a new residence in a
more modern style.

Left: Stirling Palace, seen from the south-east.

STIRLING AS AN ARMY BASE

By Defoe's time, Stirling Castle was in the hands of the army. A garrison had been stationed here from the late 1600s to suppress religious and political dissent, and military needs remained paramount for almost 300 years. Damage to remaining decoration was inevitable and the army made many changes over the centuries, such as putting in new stairs and fireplaces, raising ceilings and opening out new doors. But at least providing shelter for soldiers required that the roofs were kept watertight. And the army high command in London was in no hurry to spend money on major rebuilding to make the quarters more convenient or comfortable when the priority was artillery defences or military roads in the Highlands. A report of 1859 described the Palace as 'one of the worst barracks in the three kingdoms'.

Indeed, there were two attempts at renovation during the 1600s, one for James VI's return visit in 1617 and the other in anticipation of a possible return by Charles II in the early 1670s. These works at least kept the buildings in repair, and the detailed surviving records of the work in the 1670s provided valuable information for the Palace Project. Visitors in the early 1700s could see that the rooms were still impressive. In 1723, for example, the gentleman traveller John Macky described them as 'the noblest I ever saw in Europe' for their size and their carved woodwork. Just three years later, however, the writer Daniel Defoe reported, ominously:

'… The Palace and Royal apartments are very magnificent, but all in Decay … we thought it would be much better to pull them down than to let such Buildings sink into their own Rubbish …'

One benefit of the army presence was the military fondness for drawing plans, which were carefully filed away; it is from plans drawn in the early 1700s that we can identify the king's and queen's suites, each with what was then called its 'Garde Hall', 'Presence' and 'Bed Chamber' (corresponding to what are now called the Outer Hall, Inner Hall and Bedchamber).

Still, lack of maintenance was to exact a sad cost. In 1777 one of the carved oak roundels known as the Stirling Heads (see Chapter 7) fell and injured a soldier. In consequence, all the carved woodwork was stripped out, seemingly for sale as firewood. It was only by good fortune that some of the Heads were saved by enthusiasts and collectors, the most important being Ebenezer Brown, keeper of the Stirling prison, where many of these incomparable works of art were kept for many years.

Above: An illustration by the military draughtsman John Slezer of Stirling Castle in the 1690s. At this time, the Forework still stood at its full height and was less obscured by defensive structures to the south.

MILITARY ADAPTATIONS

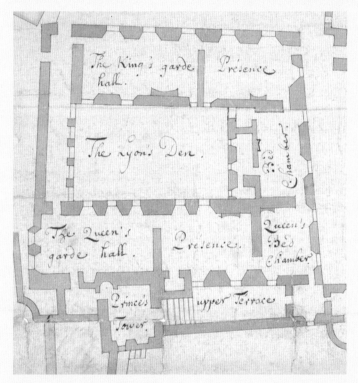

By the late 1600s, the needs of the army were forcing radical change within the Palace. In 1685, for example, both the King's and the Queen's Bedchambers were lined with timber for the storage of oatmeal. Around the same time, the stair to the upper floor was taken out and the present stairway inserted; the upper floor became a residence for the castle governor. Small scraps of wallpaper from this period have been found on the walls.

In the 1700s the Palace became barracks accommodation. During the Napoleonic Wars the pressures were particularly acute. Mezzanine floors were created so that, by the late 1820s, there were two floors of iron bedsteads for soldiers in the Palace and many more in the Great Hall. The 1841 census shows 268 people living in the castle; other army staff lived in the town but still required office space or other accommodation within the castle.

From the late 1840s, the railway brought greatly increasing numbers of visitors to Stirling. As late as the 1950s, and in spite of a century of increasing awareness of the Palace's historic importance, the apartments were still subdivided as offices and bars, with a 'night club' in the Prince's Tower.

Top: Part of a plan of Stirling Palace drawn up by the military engineer Theodore Dury in the early 1700s. The main rooms are labelled as 'Garde Hall', 'Presence' and 'Bed Chamber'.

Above: Members of The Argyll and Sutherland Highlanders drilling on the Esplanade. Stirling Castle was the regiment's depot for nearly a century.

JANE GRAHAM AND THE LOST HEADS

Jane Graham (née Ferrier) was married to General John Graham, a British hero of the American War of Independence. But she has her own claims to fame. As a young woman in Edinburgh she caught the eye of the poet Robert Burns. In 1787, he wrote 'To Miss Ferrier', describing how the mere sight of her had lifted his despondent spirits:

Do what I dought to set her free,
My saul lay in the mire;
Ye turned a neuk – I saw your e'e –
She took the wing like fire!

In later life, when her husband was deputy governor at Stirling Castle, she recognised the importance of the surviving woodwork from the Palace – the carvings now known as the Stirling Heads. They were scattered in several locations and she undertook to record what she could find.

She was an accomplished if amateur artist, and her drawings appeared in a lavish volume, *Lacunar Strevelinense*, published in 1817. This had the great benefit of drawing attention to the surviving items and raising awareness of their importance.

Some of the Heads were placed in museums. But some remained in private hands and two of these were destroyed in a fire at Dunstaffnage in 1940. For those two, Jane Graham's drawings are the only record which now survives.

Top: Jane Ferrier in her youth, an inspiration to Robert Burns.

Above: Her illustrations of the Stirling Heads depicting Mary of Guise and Henry VIII. These are the only surviving records of two Heads that were destroyed in 1940.

REVIVING THE PALACE

By the mid-1800s, as the castle's military importance diminished, its heritage value was increasingly recognised. But as late as the 1950s several of the royal chambers were subdivided to form passages and offices and it was only in 1964, after the castle finally ceased to be a military base, that major restoration could be contemplated. In the 1990s, with Stirling Castle established as a major visitor attraction, a comprehensive plan was developed which included the restoration of the Great Kitchens, the Chapel Royal and the Great Hall, culminating with the refurbishment of the Palace.

It was decided at an early stage that the project would involve recreating and displaying a set of tapestries, to be based on the Unicorn series now housed in the Cloisters Gallery in New York. It was also decided that a full set of replicas of the surviving Stirling Heads would be created and placed on the ceiling of the King's Inner Hall, while the originals would be conserved and newly displayed. Both of these parts of the project are considered in detail in this book (see Chapters 6 and 7) – though it is worth emphasising here that the process of artistic recreation has itself contributed to our understanding of how the Palace was created.

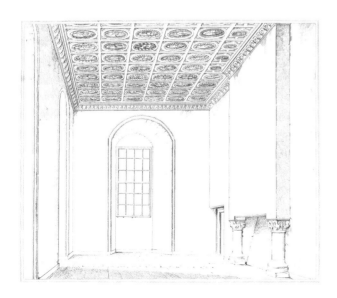

Above: An illustration from *Lacunar Strevelinense* of the Stirling Heads in their original positions on the ceiling of the King's Inner Hall.

Above: An illustration of the Palace and Great Hall by the architect Robert Billings, who carried out important repairs at Stirling Castle in the 1850s.

THE PRINCIPLES OF THE PALACE PROJECT

The aims of the Stirling Castle Palace Project went beyond creating the stunning interiors which visitors see today.

♣ Among the main aims were: the conservation and repair of the surviving historic fabric of the building; meticulous recording of the building and its context; research into the building's history and significance – in the 1500s and up to the present day; researching the meanings and significance of the building and its carved decoration.

♣ The re-presentation of the Palace was based on the surviving physical and documentary evidence, supported by reference to wider studies at a European level. There is a rationale for the inclusion of each feature and artefact.

♣ The research has been peer-reviewed by specialists from throughout the UK and France. Results are open to scrutiny and all the archaeological and historical data and research have been made freely available online (www.sparc.scran.ac.uk). Much more material will be published after the completion of the project. So the research results are a useful resource and important well beyond the project itself.

♣ It was a cardinal rule that the integrity of the building was not to be damaged by the work and only the most appropriate, high-quality materials and craftsmanship were to be used. Some compromises had to be made with materials, however. For example, it was decided not to use authentic lead-based paints as they are toxic.

♣ Inevitably, such a meticulous project was expensive, with a total cost of £12 million. However, millions of people will experience it and even more will be able to read about it. The project will remain an asset for generations to come, a long-term contribution to Scotland's culture and a beacon of excellence, showcasing Scotland's history.

CHALLENGES AND DISCOVERIES

Creating the Heads and the tapestries was a challenge indeed. But the recreation of entire interiors was a challenge of a different sort. Only the skeleton of the building remained; the load-bearing walls were standing but there was little trace of the 16th-century decoration of the interior. There are fireplaces and some of the doors from the period – but none of the ceilings or floors have survived intact. The documentary evidence included some inventories of furniture (though most are not specific to Stirling and all are probably incomplete); there were short runs of building accounts and household accounts; there were a few descriptions by visitors. Nobody who was involved in the early phases of the research was under any illusion: translating these fragments of evidence into a credible version of a 16th-century Scots royal interior was a daunting prospect.

Some information emerged quickly, clearly and convincingly – though it sometimes involved surprises! Log fires are a powerful component of our mental picture of the luxurious past. But the documentary evidence was unequivocal – while some wood was used in the kitchens, the most important fuel in all the Scots royal residences was coal. That meant that the fire-grates and fireside equipment would be those appropriate for coal rather than wood. And, at a very practical level, a cartload of coal gives a lot more heat than a cartload of wood.

Detailed recording of the surviving structure, above and below ground, underpinned the whole project. A particularly innovative aspect has been the way in which the upstanding building was investigated as a piece of archaeology, with the results integrated with the documentary and other evidence. Traditional archaeology, in which trenches are dug, and buried features and finds are revealed and recorded, has been going on within Stirling Castle for many decades and has contributed a great deal to our knowledge. But what do we mean by the 'archaeology' of an upstanding building – including its upper floors and roof structure?

Above: Archaeological excavations in the Ladies' Lookout, immediately to the west of the Palace.

Above: Most of the fires within the Palace burned coal, not wood.

GATHERING EVIDENCE

A traditional archaeologist's trench is a way of investigating change in space and in time. Which is the newer feature and what existed before it was created? Archaeologists have developed sophisticated ways of recording and classifying what they find so that, for example, layers in one trench can be related to those in another, some distance away. But, until the recent past, if the underground finds included the base of a wall then the archaeological investigation stopped at ground level; anything higher was considered to be architecture. For the purposes of the Palace Project, that artificial barrier was abandoned.

That is not to say there has been no role for architectural investigation within the project – again, this book includes a chapter on the architecture and sculpture. But archaeological recording methods have revealed a dynamic picture of the building's evolution so that we can gain a clearer impression of what it was like at any one time in its 500-year history. By showing how James V's building work was integrated with structures which already stood on parts of the site, for example, the investigation showed why the Palace's sides do not lie quite at right angles to each other.

The integrated approach also means that later changes to the building can be identified. There were 17th-century accounts for the laying of new floorboards on the upper floor and work on the roofs. Through dendrochronology (tree-ring analysis) the source of the wood was identified as the eastern Baltic area. By correlating the several strands of evidence, a richer and more informative view of the past was revealed. Armed with that, it became easier to imagine that part of the building before the new floor was laid.

Another key part of the approach was to look for comparative evidence, at what was happening elsewhere in fashionable Europe in the 1500s. Certainly, there were aspects of the Palace which were distinctively Scots – the thistles on some of the fireplaces survive as an obvious example. But cultural historians now know that much was shared between countries; it was the detail which varied. James V did not just import furniture and tapestries and clothes. He also imported ideas about what was fashionable and desirable. English or French visitors to his residences would recognise much of what they saw, in spite of the Scottishness of some of the details.

Above: A cross-section through the Queen's Lodgings, revealing (left to right) the Outer Hall, Inner Hall and Bedchamber. The upper floor and vaults are shown at top and bottom.

PRESERVING THE ORIGINAL FEATURES

Visitors will be struck by the contrast between the many highly-finished, bright and colourful surfaces in the Royal Lodgings and the bare stone of the fireplaces. Less obviously, some of the doors and their moulded stone frames are worn.

These features have been left 'as found' because they are original and so still have the potential to provide further evidence about the past. Tiny traces of paint remain on the fireplaces, but too little to indicate the overall scheme (which would also have included gilding). Even more importantly, any repainting now would damage what evidence remains – and who knows what new methods of examination might emerge in the future? So, they are left bare.

The doors consist of two layers of boards, one vertical and one horizontal, held firmly together by double-headed nails, a classic contemporary method of controlling warping of the wood before panelled doors were usual. The wood has been dated to the 1500s so these are original – though some have evidently been moved and reinstalled in other doorways at some point, for reasons which are not clear. But, at 2m wide, there is no doubt that the huge door at the main entrance from the Inner Close is where it has always been!

The windows presented a different problem. They had been fitted with sash-and-case windows – entirely wrong for the 1500s but now an integral part of the historic structure. Lateral thinking and some ingenious design work has preserved the sashes while introducing 16th-century-style shutters and half-glazed windows to the interiors.

Among the many remarkable finds in the Palace were two ritual protection marks (witch marks) as well as the conjoined letters 'AMV' (for Ave Maria Virginus or 'Hail to the Virgin Mary') and an incised marigold on the inner face of the door to the King's Closets.

Above: A detail of the fireplace in the King's Bedchamber, carved with a thistle motif.

Above: One of the half-glazed windows in the King's Bedchamber.

ACCOUNTS AND INVENTORIES

European influences were crucially important in considering some of the documentary evidence. We have only the most general descriptions for furniture, for example, though it is known that James and Mary of Guise both had high-status furniture imported from France. The accounts and inventories provide very detailed descriptions of what James V wore (though less detail for Mary) and these show that their clothes were of broadly European styles, the king's sometimes with Scots detail such as thistle trimmings. There are also detailed descriptions of some of the finest fabrics including cloth of gold and of silver. Silks (including velvets) were mainly made in Italy and imported via markets such as Antwerp and so were of the elite style of the period.

There are similarly detailed descriptions of the hangings made for new beds, both four-poster beds and those with canopies suspended from the ceiling, and the necessary bedding. 'Turkey' carpets are among the few items to originate outside Europe but they, too, would have been imported via European markets. All these must have been of the elite styles of the period. A similar range of considerations governed the choice of wall treatments and other decorative details (see Chapter 4).

One major issue was whether the Palace was finished before the king died in December 1542. Work was probably underway in 1538, some roofing work was in progress in 1541 and James and Mary of Guise were both at Stirling in April 1542. The widowed Mary and her daughter Mary Queen of Scots became regular residents from July 1543. But this does not prove that they lived in the Palace and, even if they did, was it necessarily complete?

Top: James V and Mary of Guise in a double portrait. Both wear elaborate costumes incorporating gold thread and gemstones.

Above left: A chair and cloth of estate created for the Queen's Inner Hall. The equivalent items were not produced for the King's Lodgings, since the Palace re-creation represents the period after James V's death.

Certainly, if it was finished by summer 1543, 16th-century builders must have been fast workers. For that reason, the Palace is presented as it might have been some years later, when completion seems more certain.

But with the king dead and Mary of Guise resident in the Queen's Lodgings, there was a question as to how the king's side of the Palace would be furnished and dressed. Perhaps, for the highest festivals, days of national importance such as her coronation, the infant Mary Queen of Scots would have occupied the king's side. But, on a practical, day-to-day basis she would have had a warm, convenient nursery elsewhere within the castle. In those circumstances, the lavish furnishings and fittings of the king's side would probably have been put into storage for safekeeping. So the King's Lodgings are not presented fully 'dressed'. The interpretation concentrates on the fixtures and, of course, on the replica Stirling Heads now adorning the ceiling of the King's Inner Hall.

The Stirling Heads are among the jewels of the project. The replicas are painted in authentic 16th-century style, and it is possible to make out an astonishing level of detail, even when they are so far above our heads. The original

Heads had been dispersed and displayed in various places for many years. The project has included provision for them to be brought together, studied, conserved and, in most cases, displayed in the exhibition on the upper floor. There they form part of a wider interpretation of the Palace and of 16th-century Scots royal life. And, given the inevitable access problems of a building which is almost 500 years old, fully accessible interpretation of the Palace and its occupants has also been included in the Palace vaults.

So, the project brings to life something of the astonishing magnificence of a 16th-century royal residence. Just one part of the Palace has been left almost untouched. On the west side, the passage giving access to the two Royal Lodgings has been left, stripped to bare walls, revealing in stone the changes of five centuries. It is a reminder that what we now see is a reconstruction of what might once have existed.

But the presentation of the Palace has been informed by the results of years of detailed research and painstaking scholarship. What we see is a credible vision of a splendid moment in Scotland's past, as well as a major contribution to Scotland's present.

Above: Three of the replica Stirling Heads produced for the Palace Project.

3 THE ARCHITECTURE, STATUES AND SCULPTURE

STRUCTURES AND SYMBOLISM

The architecture of the Palace was like nothing else ever seen in Scotland. While the building does have features intended to evoke medieval towers, it can justifiably be recognised as one of the finest Renaissance buildings in Britain. This fashionable royal residence was built on the orders of James V for his new queen, Mary of Guise. It is an extraordinary building, of pleasing proportions, with a fascinating stepped façade, alternating between large windows and near life-size human statues.

Looking up today from the Queen Anne Garden is as close as we can come to the view of the Palace seen by an approaching visitor in the 1500s, since Stirling Castle's former impressive main frontage was largely hidden by new defences built in the early 1700s. From the garden, the Palace looms high above us, partly obscured by the Prince's Tower and the great mass of the forewall which was the outer defensive line for much of the 1500s. Its air of military strength is enhanced by the battlemented wall-heads of the Palace itself, by James IV's great towered entrance gate and by its continuation to the east, all now much reduced. From here we can see, too, the four stone lions crowning the rooflines, one at each gable, which tell us, emphatically, that this place belongs to the king of Scots.

Left: Statues on the south façade of the Palace.

AN AWKWARD BUILDING SITE

The dramatic changes in level on the summit made it very difficult to construct substantial buildings on the castle rock. But this was a challenge relished by the architects and builders when work began around 1538. With other buildings already on the site, they had little spare room to play with as they tried to squeeze in a palace. Some clever tricks were used. For example (and unusually) the King's Bedchamber is at right-angles to the rest of the King's Lodgings, neatly bringing it side-by-side with the Queen's Bedchamber. The Palace also takes advantage of the steep slope of the ground so that the eastern end has a substantial undercroft, providing vaulted storage, while at the west the main entry is at ground level.

Even within that confined space, there is an inner courtyard, traditionally called the Lion's Den – though there is no evidence that a lion was ever really kept there. It is very plain and unornamented but the use of a hollow square is a typical device of the period. It allows for windows on two or three sides of most of the royal chambers so that these large rooms, which could so easily have been gloomy, have good natural light.

The extent to which the builders overcame the challenges of a difficult site, and their desire to create a sophisticated and unfamiliar design, become apparent when we go inside and see how stylish and well-proportioned these large, bright spaces are. True, aspects of the Palace might have looked old-fashioned by the standards of the 1540s – but this was a time when echoes of the medieval past had positive connotations of old chivalric glories. Certainly, so far as it was old-fashioned, it was not so from ignorance. There are clear signs of contemporary French and Italian influence ahead of anything in England at the time. But there was no attempt to ape foreign styles either; the Scots had a long tradition of stone-built architecture and had no reason to hide the building's Scots accents. Again, to have something vernacular and local was a part of the message, an expression of national self-confidence. A mix of old and new, of local and international, was precisely in line with the tastes of the time.

Above: The Lion's Den, the courtyard at the centre of the Palace, designed to allow light in to its windows.

STONE CONSERVATION: CHRISTA GERDWILKER

As part of the Palace Project, Historic Scotland staff undertook the vital task of recording and conserving the outside of the Palace, including the sculptures and other decorative details. Scaffolding was in place for several months.

Christa Gerdwilker, one of the stone conservation team, explains. 'We work within standard conservation guidelines and ethics,' she says. 'We don't aim to return the Palace to its original state but to use minimal and reversible intervention, to stabilise the stonework and reduce future deterioration.'

Some moss and lichen growth was removed with water and soft brushes, mainly to ascertain the state of the underlying stone; corrosive bird droppings were removed with equally gentle methods. Cracks and fissures in the stonework can be injected with removable acrylic resins followed by pointing with an appropriate, colour-matched mortar. Areas of softening and crumbling stone were treated with consolidants called silanes. Corroded metal fixings, which had damaged the stonework, had been replaced many years ago.

Some statues required more work than others, Christa explains. 'The stone of Saturn's legs contained pockets of softer minerals which have suffered accelerated erosion. We consolidated these areas by locally injecting acrylic resin and pointing cracks and fissures with acrylic mortar.' But most of the statues, made of good though workable stone, required surprisingly little work. James V himself, the team were pleased to find, needed only to have some bird droppings removed from his crown.

Above: Christa Gerdwilker working at Dunadd hillfort in Kilmartin Glen, Argyll.

UNDERSTANDING THE STATUES

The Palace is also one of the most highly embellished buildings of its period in Britain, with over 200 stone figures and busts, including no fewer than 159 astonishingly diverse *putti* (or cherubs). New research has helped us understand this remarkable building – though there are still plenty of mysteries for future researchers to investigate.

Returning to the south front and again looking up at the Palace, we see four stone figures at the wall-head, against the battlements. They are men-at-arms: one holds a sword, one a crossbow, one a hand-gun; the other fires a gun into the air. There were similar armed figures on the wall-heads at James V's contemporary palace at Falkland; while among the real, flesh-and-blood garrison of Stirling Castle in the 1500s were the garitours – the watchers on the wall-heads.

But these four stone figures are more than a symbolic, unblinking reinforcement to that human watch. For in Gavin Douglas's allegorical poem *Palace of Honour* (1501) the garitour was 'Lawtie' – a Scots word for loyalty. The garitour of another of his idealised palaces was

'Fair Calling', while another banished envy and covetousness. Our four statues might therefore represent a moral defence of the Palace as well as a military one. As we will see, all the external sculpture is rich in meaning.

Below each of the four soldiers is another larger figure. One of these is instantly recognisable: an androgynous Devil, winged and horned with pendulous breasts, cloven feet and a mask-like face on its belly. The other three are nude figures, a girl and two boys, two of whom hold objects in their hands with a gesture more like putting the shot than preparing to throw a weapon. None of these figures need indicate aggression. In 1520, Henry VIII built a temporary palace in Calais for his meeting with Francis I of France, adorning it with images of men of war casting stones and shooting guns, yet the meeting was a major diplomatic initiative, with both kings wishing to emphasise friendship. There may be an underlying theme of 'chaos' or, like the wall-head men-at-arms, these figures may be engaged in a moral struggle between the inner world of the Palace and the outer world, including distant England, which they face.

Above: A man-at-arms, or garitour, holding a sword.

Above: A garitour holding a crossbow.

Above: A garitour firing a gun into the air.

Above: A garitour with a hand-gun and classical face-shield.

Top: A Devil and two of the figures flanking him on the south façade.

Above: The Field of the Cloth of Gold, a temporary palace built by Henry VIII in Calais for his meeting with Francis I of France in 1520. Although the meeting was amicable, martial figures can be seen on the palace's roof, as on the south façade of Stirling Palace.

THE NORTH FAÇADE

The north façade, seen from the Inner Close with its higher ground-level, is much less dominating than the south. Though the rhythm of windows, columns and statues is the same as on the south, it gives a very different overall impression. There are no towers as reminders of the medieval past; the windows and statues are closer to us and so seem larger. And, since this was a view only seen by those who were within the castle gates, it was a view for friends and allies.

Research for the Palace Project has shown that the message of this façade is very different from that of the south. The one surviving wall-head figure is not a soldier but a naked cherub playing a pipe; nor are the main statues below about war or threat. Rather, this façade introduces ideas of peace and plenty and of a new Golden Age presided over by James V himself, present on the corner at the viewer's extreme left. Not only does his plinth rise from a lion, but above him is another lion holding a crown above his head and a label with the king's monogram, 'I5' (Iacobus is the Latin form of James). His long beard might be intended to imply the wisdom of an Old Testament prophet.

By good fortune, three of the other figures on the north and east façades are similar to engravings published by the German artist Hans Burgkmair earlier in the 1500s. But there are discrepancies between the prints and the statues, which have puzzled scholars for decades. Research for the project has considerably advanced our understanding of them.

One of the north façade statues is loosely based on a figure Burgkmair labels as Venus. She is further identified in Burgkmair's engraving by the dart under her left arm, while a Cupid (with his own tiny bow and arrows) dances on the globe which she holds in her right hand. These were among the attributes of Venus as goddess of love in the ancient world. Our statue does have a dart but she wears decorated greaves (shin guards) absent in the print, and there is no sign that there was ever a Cupid on her globe. This suggests that she is Venus Armata, a Venus who has triumphed over Mars (the god of war) whose weapons she now uses as playthings. This was an idea familiar to James's contemporaries. Henry VIII had a writing desk which paired this same engraving with the corresponding image of Mars, to celebrate the peace associated with an idealised royal marriage.

Above: The north façade of the Palace, on which James V's own statue appears alongside gods of the Classical world.

In this form, as a sign of concord or peace, Venus has no need of Cupid. And some of the other statues also lack some (or even all) of their traditional attributes because of the meaning assigned to them in the Palace scheme. A case in point is the figure to the right of Venus. He is a middle-aged man with a beard and is roughly based on another of Burgkmair's engravings, identified as the Roman god Saturn. The bearded Saturn in the engraving holds a scythe in his right hand, representing Time, which forever destroys but is forever new.

The statue has no scythe, however, and instead presents Saturn as the ruler of the Golden Age. This was imagined both as a real, historical time in the past and as something which could be achieved again in the future. In the Golden Age, peace, plenty and harmony would flow from just and wise rule. So, to use images of Saturn in connection with the start of a new reign or a royal marriage was to suggest that the justice and wisdom of this particular ruler would see the return of the Golden Age. Indeed, the newly-crowned Henry II of France was greeted by imagery of the Golden Age at his entry to Lyons on 1548, to Paris in 1549 and to Rouen in 1550, where a statue of Saturn was placed above the town gate.

Saturn can be seen as the good and just ruler of a contented people. With peace and concord represented by Venus Armata, and with the Golden Age represented by Saturn, it begins to appear that this whole façade might have an overall message about good government.

Top: Hans Burgkmair's engraving of Saturn, published around 1520.

Above: The statue of Saturn on the Palace's north façade.

Top: Burgkmair's engraving of Venus.

Above: The statue of Venus, again showing Burgkmair's influence.

To the right of Saturn is a young woman, her slight and swirling drapery conveying a real sense of movement. Saturn (whose many associations include agriculture) had married the Roman goddess of the earth (who was also his sister), known as Flora. Here she holds a Cornucopia or 'horn of plenty' and she exemplifies Abundance, always associated with the Golden Age and its exemplary government and ruler. It is possible that the statue is based on engravings of Roman sculptures, some newly excavated at the Forum in Rome, published in the early 1530s, close to the date when work on the Palace began.

Finally, next to the king, we see a young man in Classical breastplate and greaves, holding a cup in his right hand. He is most probably Ganymede, the youthful and beautiful cup-bearer to the gods. If that is correct, he might indicate the perpetual youth to be enjoyed by all in the forthcoming Golden Age.

Right: The statue identified as Ganymede, cup-bearer of the Classical gods.

THE EAST FAÇADE

On the east façade, several of the figures are badly damaged, making interpretation more difficult. Two of the wall-head figures appear to hold musical instruments; the two others (both damaged, nude males) appear to have held stone ribbons. These ribbons probably once had inscriptions which must have helped explain the overall meaning but which have now vanished. The figure of St Michael trampling Satan, like James himself, has been placed in a pivotal position on the corner, uniting the sculptural tableaux on the east and south façades. The chapel at Stirling was dedicated to St Michael, but his main importance here may be that he was patron of the French order of chivalry of which James V was a member.

Another key figure is the Roman god Jupiter, again based on one of Burgkmair's engravings. Others are identified, with greater or lesser degrees of certainty, as Venus Pudica (a more earthly form of the goddess of love), Orpheus (a mythical poet and musician who charmed the Underworld with his lyre) and Fergus (a king from Scotland's ancient past).

The thread connecting this very mixed collection is law and rational good government. For 16th-century scholars, Jupiter was not just the supreme god of the ancient world; he also governed human reason. According to ancient myth, Fergus had introduced law into Scotland. Orpheus, a bringer of peace, has a role similar to Abundance on the north façade, representing the outcome of just and responsible rule.

Above right: An armorial panel from the outer gateway at Linlithgow Palace, representing James V's membership of the French chivalric order of St Michael.

Above: The headless statue of St Michael trampling Satan underfoot on the Palace's east façade.

Above (clockwise from top left): The statue of Venus Pudica; another headless statue, probably Jupiter; a statue of Orpheus, the heroic poet and musician; the torso and legs of a figure tentatively identified as King Fergus.

THE PUTTI – PEACE, LOVE AND HEAVENLY REJOICING

Figures of small children have been used to decorate tombs and buildings since at least the early Christian centuries. They were particularly fashionable between the 1500s and 1800s, when they also appeared widely in paintings. They are given various names, including *putti* (the plural form of the Italian *putto*) and cherubs. They are often male, naked and winged, sometimes reduced to just head and wings.

Two of the surviving Stirling Heads are full-length *putti*, dancing with ribbons. Winged cherub heads also appear on the breasts of several of the Heads. Winged heads are also the most numerous form found among the astonishing 159 *putti* on the outside of the Palace.

But what messages were these figures intended to convey? *Putti* have meanings as varied as their appearance. Sometimes, as when they

accompany the heavenward journey of a saint, they signify heavenly rejoicing. In other contexts they signify love, peace or even simple fun. But it is more difficult to interpret these figures, which are now isolated from their context.

One suggestion is that they were symbolic 'guardians', protecting the royal residents while observing and rewarding the just deeds of the court below. Another is that they encouraged the prince to improve his land through virtue and by building. It has even been suggested that those on the exterior might represent the descendants of James V and Mary of Guise – presumably extended into a very distant future. But there are numerous other possibilities and the question remains as one of the many mysteries of the Palace.

Above: Stirling Head 37, one of two with a *putto* as main subject.

Above left: A winged cherub head carved on the Palace exterior.

Above right: A *putto* displayed on the breast of a statue on the Palace exterior.

THE WEST FAÇADE

There is a sharp contrast between the three highly ornamented façades with their big windows and the west side, overlooking the park. Seen from below, it provides the most iconic view of Stirling Castle, high on its cliff. Sadly, the west range and gallery which used to ornament this façade collapsed in the early 1600s. It would have provided wonderful views over the gardens, park and surrounding countryside. The site was later used for more pragmatic purposes: latrines and gun emplacements.

The sculpture on the Palace exterior is sometimes seen as crude: in the 1700s it was described as 'grotesque'. Even the figure of Abundance – with its sense of movement and lightness by far the 'best' of the statues – is rough by comparison with the finest Classical or Renaissance work. But Burgkmair and some other northern European artists rejected what they

saw as the over-delicate sentimentality of some of their contemporaries, a trend inevitably followed by the French-led sculptors at Stirling.

Indeed, it might reasonably be wondered, was it all so sophisticated that nobody at court could ever have grasped its meaning? Certainly educated contemporaries were more familiar with the attributes of Classical figures than we are today. And perhaps there was a deliberate intention to be erudite, partly to show off but also so that even the cognoscenti had to ponder and discuss (the very best way to reinforce a lesson, as any teacher knows!). Nor did they judge with our 21st-century taste; the southern approach, with its medieval-looking towers and its obviously military intent, was described as 'the whole outward beauty' of Stirling Castle in the 1580s.

Above: Stirling Castle from the south-west. To the right is the Palace's undecorated west face; to the left is the King's Old Building, dating from the 1490s.

Much, too, has changed. The statues have been damaged or eroded. They would once have been painted in bright colours; and even the walls of the Palace would have been lime-washed. What we can now do, thanks to the new research, is look at the outside as well as the inside of the Palace and see something of the ambition which drove forward the scheme, read more of the messages the building was intended to convey, and better appreciate the quality and significance of the work, all informed by strong European contacts.

Above: A selection of human figures projecting from column bases and other architectural features of the Palace.

BEHIND THE GRAND DESIGN – THE BUILDERS AND CARVERS

The building of the Palace was initially led by the king's master of works, Sir James Hamilton of Finnart, followed by Sir James Nicolson from August 1540 when Finnart was executed for treason. Nicolson was succeeded a year later by Robert Robertson, who had worked his way up from being a joiner and had made panelling and ceilings for the Palace.

The scale of some of the payments for wages, for example in the summer of 1541, indicate that a very large team, comprising a wide variety of trades, was busy on the Palace. There was an existing tradition in Scotland of French and Flemish craftsmen employed on royal building works. More French craftsmen were recruited by James V during his months in France in 1536, while others arrived in the service of Mary of Guise. They were responsible for the French influence on the design of the Palace, and no doubt provided the Continental flavour seen in the exterior sculpture and wood carving, with teams of local craftsmen working under them. Included among the recorded craftsmen were Moses Martin, a French stonemason, and Pierre Quesnel, a decorative and portrait painter.

Above: The coat of arms of Sir James Hamilton of Finnart, with antelope supporters. Though he won James V's favour and served as his master of works, he was convicted of treason and executed in 1540.

' Do equal Justice both to great and small
And be example to thy people all,
Exercising virtuous deeds honourable.
Be not a wretch, whatever may befall.
To that unhappy vice, if thou be thrall,
To all men thou shalt be abominable.
Kings nor knights are never suitable
To rule people, be they not liberal:
Was never yet no wretch to honour able.'

Sir David Lyndsay, 'The Exhortation to the
King's Grace', written for James V around 1530

Above: The statue of James V at the
north-east corner of the Palace.

Top: The statue is sheltered by a cusped arch, surmounted by a lion holding the crown and James's monogram 'I5'.

Above: A female figure protrudes from lower down the column on which James's statue stands.

Top left: Venus, goddess of love, as portrayed on the north façade.

Above left: A statue on the north façade probably representing Ganymede, cup-bearer to the gods.

Above: Saturn, god of time and agriculture, as portrayed on the north façade.

Left: Perhaps the most skilfully executed of the deity statues, this figure on the north façade probably represents Abundance.

Above: A Devil figure which dominates the exterior
south façade of the Palace.

Above: A tormented-looking figure at the
base of the Devil's statue.

Above: The south wall of the Palace, the façade visible
to anyone approaching the castle from the town.

This page: A digital reconstruction of the north façade as it
may have looked when completed in the 1540s. It is very likely
that the statues and other elements would have been painted
in bright colours.

4 FURNISHINGS, WALLS AND FITTINGS
FORMALITY AND FUNCTION

During the 1400s, European courts had begun to adopt new standards of magnificence and splendour. This was particularly apparent in the elaborate and often symbolic detailing and in the use of luxurious fabrics and rich and expensive dyes to produce astonishingly bright colours. James IV had adopted something of the new styles, but James V did so wholeheartedly – and that is reflected in the opulence of the interiors now seen in the Palace.

The inner spaces, the more intimate apartments, have the more lavish decoration and furnishing. That said, all the spaces were more or less adaptable and could be used for meetings, for eating or for social or other activities as need arose. That fluidity is reflected in the sparseness of the furniture, much of which could be readily moved from room to room or even between residences. Even the great state bed, huge and richly dressed to reflect its prestige, could perhaps have been broken down for transport.

Opposite: The prayer table and triptych in the Queen's Bedchamber.

FABRICS AND FURNISHINGS

It is on the walls and ceilings that many of the dynastic, religious and patriotic messages appear, whether carved, painted or applied as hanging fabrics. Fabrics produce much of the decorative effect, reflecting the huge cost and prestige of the finest and heaviest materials. Even where richly carved, the furniture was often used to display fabrics, from silk drapes to ornate cushions, carpets and hangings.

A glance around the queen's apartments reveals that these three very large rooms have just three chairs between them. The chairs are very handsome items, with their cross-frame structure, red velvet and silk fringes. James V imported chairs of this sort from France, and the king and queen sat on similar chairs at her coronation. But there would be no lounging about on one of these, no curling up with a good book. They are 'sit up straight' chairs and, like so much of the furniture, made more for formality than for comfort. In this case, their positions – under cloths of estate, with two of them raised on daises – underscore their importance.

But the chairs are not the only seats. There are six low stools in the Queen's Inner Hall; they are covered but are clearly much less formal than the chairs, lower down and lower-status. And there are benches or forms in the Outer Hall. An inventory of 1542 includes six stools for women to sit on, which were covered with embroidered fabric, while benches feature in several of the lists. The chairs and stools you now see have been adapted from authentic 16th-century originals, which either survive or appear in illustrations.

Chairs did not become common, even in quite grand houses, until well into the 1600s and even then they remained rather prestigious items. Most people would never sit on anything grander than a stool or bench. Stools and benches for attendants and others were almost essential since one of the most characteristic activities of the 16th-century court was waiting. Waiting for something to happen, waiting for the queen to arrive or to go out, to go to dinner or to take the air. Then there would be a sudden flurry of activity before the waiting resumed. In that way, the benches and stools tell us as much as the chairs about the life of the court – and the uncovered benches speak clearly of long, uncomfortable tedium.

Above: The chair of state in the Queen's Bedchamber. A canopy is suspended above it, from which hangs the cloth of estate.

Placing the two chairs under cloths of estate, with canopies and valances, further focuses attention; only the queen would usually enter the space under the canopies, others keeping a respectful distance. The cloths of estate are decorated with the arms of Mary of Guise as Queen of Scotland (see panel on heraldry, page 21), a proud proclamation of her ancestry, now linked to Scotland's royal line. And the arms, unlike the queen, can be there 24 hours a day, silently representing her in her absence.

Above: A 16th-century Turkish carpet from the Victoria and Albert Museum in London, used as a model for one of the Palace carpets.

In the Inner Hall, where the queen would have received important visitors, the focus on the chair is further heightened by its being on a raised dais, itself covered with a splendid Turkey carpet, as carpets from western Asia were called at this time. Early in the century, there are records of rushes used to strew the floors, but it is probably no accident that these vanish as records of carpets for floors become more common. The carpets were far too valuable to be used on the floors where ordinary people might walk – and it is striking that shoes for the king as well as the queen were often made of velvet, silk or other fine and soft material. Following European style, there is a carpet on the floor beside the bed. In 1565, a new Turkey carpet was laid beside Mary Queen of Scots' bed 'at the queen's command'. The previous one had been removed. Of course, the carpet was a display and, like the cloths of estate, carpets on floors marked exclusive areas. But a carpet beside the bed had the practical benefit of keeping the queen's bare feet off the cold floor.

Carpets were so exotic that they were as often found on tables as on floors, like the one on the 'chamber board' in the Queen's Bedchamber. All these fabulous carpets have been specially woven for the project, based on contemporary examples now in the Victoria and Albert Museum, though modified to suit the dimensions and conditions at Stirling.

Above: One of the cross-frame chairs of state commissioned as part of the Palace Project.

FABRICS: VIVIENNE SWATRIDGE

Vivienne Swatridge, who has researched and overseen production of the soft furnishings used in the Palace Project, wants to dispel a myth. 'Early fabrics are not crude,' she says with emphasis. 'They are often more complex in construction than achievable on modern looms.' So, though most of the fabrics for the project have been specially woven on computer-programmed looms, weaving requires intense supervision and far less is produced per day than with a plain-weave fabric.

Vivienne has spent long hours, too, studying archive fabrics, where a seam or fold has protected the original vibrancy of vegetable dyes from light, in order to gain exact colour matches. But modern chemical dyes have been used for the project, as they are capable of achieving any colour or shade and are less likely to fade over time as natural ones did.

Vivienne's personal favourite amongst the many fabrics produced are the wonderful hangings of silk and linen created for the Queen's Bedchamber, 'The design evolution is thrilling and I'm really delighted with the results,' she says.

She emphasises, too, how important fabrics were in the past. Today furnishings can be 'a frivolity' but in the past 'they were hugely expensive, highly valued, kept and recycled.'

'People might have a set of chairs covered all in one colour,' she explains, 'but they would not necessarily worry about matching other furnishings elsewhere in the room.' So, it isn't an oversight that the violets and purples in the Queen's Bedchamber do not exactly match. That is how it was likely to have been.

Above: Vivienne Swatridge working with a computer-programmed loom.

EMBROIDERY: MALCOLM LOCHHEAD AND LIZ BOULTON

Among the staff of James V's royal wardrobe department were the browdsters, professional embroiders who undertook a wide range of complex work. Two embroidered cloths of estate, showing the coat of arms of Mary of Guise as queen of Scotland, have been designed for the Palace Project by Professor Malcolm Lochhead and executed by three members of the Embroiderers' Guild.

The designs are based on a painting now at Falkland Palace. One is just under 1m across and the other 1.5m. Embroiderer Liz Boulton enjoys working on this large scale. 'It is much bigger than for a domestic setting. It's nice to have the budget to select the very expensive threads and the pearls, too.'

The larger areas, such as the unicorn and 'falcon' supporters, are made of fine leather. Malcolm says, 'Obviously, real beasts don't stand in these postures. So the faces and bodies are on the stylised side of realistic.'

With so much to do, the tasks were divided between the embroiderers. 'It's all put together like a jigsaw at the end,' says Malcolm. But that demands careful co-ordination to ensure uniform styles, and the whole team met regularly as work progressed.

Liz Boulton appreciates the benefits of modern lighting, spectacles and much better needles than in the 1500s. But, she says, 'In some ways, the traditional materials are our comfort zone. We know how they will behave.' And she rejoices that she is part of a long tradition and is excited that people may still be looking at her work several centuries from now.

Above: Malcolm Lochhead with Liz Boulton (far right) and other members of the embroidery team, working on designs for the Palace.

LIGHTING AND HEATING

There is a range of candlesticks and stands, some of silver, some sturdy wrought-iron and the simplest of wood or brass, all of contemporary types. Having lots of candles allowed the life of the court to continue after dark. It was possible to read, to dance or to hold a conversation across the room – a simple brass candlestick could be moved to light a particular point of interest, a game of chess or a book, perhaps. Other types could be raised and lowered with a pulley as required and some were fixed so they would not be readily knocked over during the dancing. Nowadays, when we flick a switch and bright light appears as if by magic, it is difficult to grasp how impressive this abundance of lights was, at a time when expensive candles were routinely kept under lock and key and everyone saved candle-ends. The court did not just shine metaphorically but with real, physical light, in turn reflected from glittering silver and mirrors, silks, jewels and cloth of gold.

The importance of fires can hardly be exaggerated either, though even in the Scottish winter it was not just their welcome heat which mattered but the cheery glow, supplementing the candles, giving a focal point in the rooms. The king and queen both had departments within their households which organised the fuel supplies, with staff dedicated to look after the fires.

Above: A 16th-century candlestick from the Victoria and Albert Museum in London, on which candlesticks in the Palace were based.

In the Outer Halls, the fires are of wood (which was also used in the kitchens); the equipment is also for wood fires and includes firedogs, to prevent logs rolling out into the room. But the documentary evidence is that most of the other fires were of coal. Coal requires a draft from below or it will not burn, so the fire is held in a raised fire basket. There is a fireback to reflect heat into the room and protect the stone, with a shovel, poker and tongs for managing the fire. All this equipment is wrought iron and, as would be the case in the 16th century, has been specially made. The designs of rare surviving examples have been modified to conform to Scots conditions, with appropriate heraldry.

The two firescreens (the one in the Queen's Bedchamber with heraldic painting but both based on a late-15th-century example) are very evocative of the way in which people sat around open fires, the highest-status person closest to the fire. There the radiant heat could be quite uncomfortable and perhaps even scorch clothes, so the screen provided some protection. Of course, further away, in these large rooms, it must sometimes have been quite chilly and we can imagine rivalry between the attendants and resentments at being squeezed to the back, perhaps a particular difficulty for some of the younger ones, who were only children.

Above: A reconstruction illustration shows Mary of Guise
and members of her court relaxing around the fireplace
in the Queen's Inner Hall.

Above: An illustration from Henry VIII's psalter (a book of Psalms)
produced around 1540 shows the English king seated on a
cross-frame chair in his richly furnished bedchamber.

THE QUEEN'S BED

Beds were of such importance that one is even listed with the jewellery. Bed frames were made of good-quality wood and sometimes carved, but the luxurious fabric hangings are particularly impressive. By the 1540s the Scots royal households had several state beds. The very finest was dressed with cloth of gold but there were 'themed' beds too, and James V had a red velvet bed-hanging decorated with 'The Story of the Life of Man Compared with a Hart' (i.e. a stag) in raised work in silver and gold, a theme that is echoed in the Unicorn tapestries.

The bed presented in the Queen's Bedchamber is based on the detailed description of one which had belonged to Mary of Guise and was transferred to Mary, her daughter, in 1561. It has been chosen because the parts of the hangings described confirm that the bed was of this four-poster type. Its hangings were of violet-brown velvet, with gold and silver braided trimmings, known as *passementerie*. It had a roof piece, head piece and curtains of violet damask without fringes. This bed had a dramatic later history. Mary gave it to her second husband Henry Stewart, Lord Darnley, and it was destroyed on the night he was murdered in 1567.

Above: Henry Stewart, Lord Darnley, second husband of Mary Queen of Scots. The bed in which he was sleeping on the night of his assassination had originally been owned by Mary of Guise.

There are cupboards in both the Queen's Inner Hall and her Bedchamber. They would have been used to display fine glassware, silver or even gold plate, but probably only when the queen was receiving official visitors whom she wished to impress. Otherwise, the valuables could be locked securely away inside, though the cupboard itself would always be a handsome item. We would expect there to be a more robust cupboard or buffet in the Outer Hall when it was in regular use; the food, brought from the kitchen, would be placed on the buffet before being offered to the diners.

Above: The bed created for the Queen's Bedchamber, based on a detailed description of Mary of Guise's bed.

OTHER FURNITURE

We know that there was an armoire (standing closet) in the queen's apartments because a payment was recorded for repairs to the hinges in 1558. The replica on display today is based on a contemporary example in the collection of the National Museums Scotland. The medallion head decoration on the doors is based on examples in the Smith Art Gallery and Museum in Stirling, with the addition of a Madonna and Child. The armoire would have been used to store clothes, a supplement to a much larger wardrobe department elsewhere.

There is a coffer or chest in the Queen's Bedchamber, made of beautifully carved walnut wood. The queen might have used it to store small, valuable or personal items and, since it is so much smaller than the armoire, it could accompany her on her travels. Coffers were used to transport the queen's personal possessions – and those of her attendants – on their frequent travels, though most would have been much simpler than this.

Finally, we come to the little prayer desk where the queen would have made her personal and private devotions, though she would also have attended Mass regularly in a public or semi-public manner. The painting on three panels (known as a triptych) could be closed to protect the painted surfaces if it was to be transported. See panel on page 72.

Above: Two of a series of carved panels found at Stirling Castle and now held in the town's Smith Art Gallery and Museum. They were used as the basis of the carved panels on the queen's armoire.

Above: A 16th-century armoire from the collection of the National Museums Scotland, on which the queen's armoire in the Palace is modelled.

Above: The armoire in the Queen's Bedchamber, based on a
contemporary one held by the National Museums Scotland.

TRIPTYCH: OWEN DAVISON

Piety, like so much of 16th-century royal life, could be largely a public affair and it was essential not to be seen to be lacking in religious devotion. But for many people, it was also deeply felt and personal. Owen Davison, who painted the triptych in the Queen's Bedchamber, kept this in mind when designing and creating it.

'The central image is the Madonna and Child,' he says. 'The Virgin Mary was Mary of Guise's own name saint. And she is flanked by St Cecilia, patron saint of music, on whose festival she was born and by St Clare, patron saint of the convent where she was educated. These were redolent images for her, not least as she would have brought the painting with her from France.' Mary had four sons before giving birth to Mary Queen of Scots: two by her first husband the Duke of Longueville, then two by James V. The youngest three all died in infancy, but her eldest boy, Francis, corresponded with her from France. 'So', Owen points out, 'the Virgin and Child must have been a reminder for her of her own children – the dead as well as the living.'

The general style of the triptych is that of Joos van Cleve, a Flemish painter of the early 1500s, whose work shows strong Italian influences. Owen has come to admire him greatly, particularly his treatment of fabrics, and he has used the traditional methods of the period.

Owen's colleague, gilder Colleen Donaldson, first prepared the surface with gesso (a 'plaster' made of natural glue and chalk) to give a flawlessly smooth surface. Owen then transferred his drawing to the surface, painting the initial stages in egg tempera and then applying the oil paint, returning to tempera for fine detail.

Mary of Guise might have prayed several times a day before this sort of image, using it to focus her thoughts and her worship. She could use these quiet moments to retreat from the hurly-burly of court life and politics into a private space, sharing her thoughts only with God and the saints.

Top: Owen Davison at work on the triptych.

Above: A detail of the Madonna and Child.

FURNITURE: KEN PETERKIN

Ken Peterkin, who has been responsible for the making of the furniture for the Palace Project, has carefully studied the rare, original pieces on which it is based. 'It's interesting that they are not particularly well-designed and give the impression that aspects of the work were afterthoughts,' he says. He wonders if the makers worked from just a rough sketch and solved the problems as they went along.

In any case, they were really only concerned with the parts of the work which would be seen; the backs and hidden parts could be 'quite rough'. This is understandable since the furniture was, first and foremost, for display. That is why seemingly 'functional' fittings, such as hinges, are so ornate and prominent, Ken explains.

After initial machining, most of the work was carried out by hand, as it would have been originally. And Ken emphasises the fascination of bringing together the range of skills to produce these complex pieces – carvers, gilders, painters, blacksmiths and others, who all need to work together.

But, Ken explains, these are not museum pieces, which have been used for centuries, scratched and damaged. 'There are uncertainties about the finishes used in the mid-16th century,' he says. 'But this furniture is presented as new.' James V did not furnish his stylish modern palace with antiques!

Above and above right: Ken Peterkin at his studio.

WALL DECORATION

There was a potentially wide range of wall-coverings available. The Palace Project team thought that the balance of evidence was against wooden panelling on the lower walls with tapestry above. An important clue for the choice of style for most of the apartments was a comment made in 1538 by the Italian humanist scholar Giovanni Ferrerio, who was familiar with the Scottish court and elite houses, that 'the lighter style' of painting was becoming fashionable in Scotland. The 'lighter style' can be identified as what is now called 'antique' or 'grotesque' painting (see panel, page 76).

There are surviving examples in Scotland and the style is also well-represented in contemporary pattern books. The King's Inner Hall replicates patterns from Mary's own apartments at Holyrood. The best surviving 16th-century wall painting in Scotland is at Kinneil, the house of James Hamilton, 2nd Earl of Arran, who governed Scotland as regent during Mary's childhood. The designs for the Queen's Outer Hall, for example, are derived from the friezes in the so-called Parable Room at Kinneil. Other examples are from English and French sites.

Above: An engraving by Robert Billings of Mary's bedchamber at the Palace of Holyroodhouse in Edinburgh. Patterns from the queen's suite at Holyrood were used in the King's Inner Hall at Stirling.

Above left: A detail of the wall-painting in the King's Inner Hall.

Above right: The 'Parable Room' at Kinneil House, whose wall-paintings inspired the décor of the Queen's Outer Hall.

The Unicorn tapestries (see Chapter 6) hang in the Queen's Inner Hall, where the full sequence of seven will be in place from 2013. The tapestries will conceal much of the walls in this room for much of the time. However, even the whole set will not fully cover the walls, and the tapestries will sometimes have to be removed for maintenance.

For this reason the walls have been painted with drapery in a *trompe l'oeil* style (from the French, meaning 'trick the eye'). This is a technique often associated with grotesque painting, in which a two-dimensional surface is made to appear three-dimensional. The effect is particularly notable at the doorways, where real drapery would be tied back, and at the top, where it would hang away from the wall. The pattern is loosely based on a floral motif which appears, with subtle variations, on the fireplace in the Queen's Bedchamber and the columns of several of the external statues.

The frieze in the Queen's Inner Hall above the painting and tapestry levels is painted with Latin texts taken from the Old Testament book of Ecclesiastes. These include 'For every thing there is a season', 'A time to be born and a time to die' and 'A time to break down and a time to build up'. Other painted mottoes in this room include 'Vyve le Roi' ('Long Live the King' in 16th-century French) and the monograms of James V and Mary of Guise.

Top: The Unicorn tapestries in the Queen's Inner Hall.

Above: A detail of the paintwork in the Queen's Inner Hall.

Above: The fireplace in the Queen's Bedchamber. Its floral harebell motif has been echoed in the wall-painting of the Queen's Inner Hall.

BEAUTY AND THE GROTESQUE

Head 16 shows a noblewoman wearing a fashionable French hood. The embroidery on the square-cut border of her bodice is of a 'grotesque' pattern, a style which was very popular in the Renaissance period and which was used in many different media.

Grotesque patterns had quickly become the favourite form of 'antique' work from the late 1400s, following the rediscovery of ancient Roman examples in the grottoes beneath the ruins, hence the 'grotesque' description. Printed pattern books were important for the rapid spread of the fashion in the 1500s.

The essence of the style was transformation and an indulgence in fantastical, writhing forms. So fronds turn into fierce beasts, serpents develop goat's feet, and hybrid creatures abound. It plays with our perceptions, perhaps using false architectural features to create strange perspectives. In media from printed books to architecture, grotesque design was often used as a framing device.

Its use was well-known in Scotland by the 1530s. James V had tapestries of 'antik' work and at the time of his death he even had a gown with buttons with grotesque enamelled decoration.

Above: Head 16, showing a noblewoman wearing a French hood and a square-cut bodice embroidered with a grotesque pattern.

Above: A grotesque motif incorporated into the wall-painting in the Queen's Bedchamber.

In the Queen's Bedchamber, where the frieze and window recesses are painted with grotesque work, the lower walls are covered almost to the floor with hangings of alternating bands of violet and green brocaded cloth, again with 'grotesque' designs. The inspiration for this treatment is a fresco of about 1520 showing a banquet at Malpaga Castle, near Bergamo, Italy.

There is no direct evidence of the floors in the royal suite at Stirling. These might have included tiles, boards and stone. For the Palace Project, a pragmatic decision was taken to simply use hard-wearing stone.

Above: The fresco at Malpaga Castle that inspired the decoration of the Queen's Bedchamber.

PAINTWORK: JOHN NEVIN

When John Nevin began working with paint in the 1960s, some paints were still being made much as they would have been in the 1500s. All the paints for walls, ceilings, heads and other surfaces at Stirling have had to be compounded on site by traditional methods. 'For the paint for the walls, we used rabbit skins to make size, a sort of glue which acts as the binder. Then we added the pigments to get the colour.' Sometimes substitute pigments had to be used – replacing toxic white lead, for example – but wherever possible authentic pigments were used too.

Many people will be surprised by how bright the colours are. But, John explains, 'Think how bright the colours are in illuminated manuscripts and tapestries. And then allow for 500 years of fading, damage and soot from candles and fires. The colours were brilliant when they were new and that is the effect we have aimed for.'

Another surprise is that John and his team spent weeks high on scaffolding, to paint the Stirling Heads in their new positions, looking close-up at the work above them. But, John explains, if they had been painted before they were in place, damage would have been inevitable and lots of touching-up would have been needed.

Some members of John's team were recruited from France where there is more demand for skills in this kind of decorative painting. And of course this mirrors the situation when the Palace was first decorated, with French painters working alongside and teaching Scots.

Sometimes very simple things are the most challenging. 'Look at the green-on-white work in the Queen's Bedchamber. It's very straightforward. But the slightest mistake would show up much more than with something more complex. I am proud of everything we have done,' John says.

Above: John Nevin in his studio.

Above: John Nevin and his son Mark at work in the Palace.

PAINTWORK: GRACIELA AINSWORTH

Above: Graciela Ainsworth at work on Head 5.

Working on the painting alongside John Nevin were Graciela Ainsworth and her team. They all have fine art training, with special expertise in conservation work, and bring both aspects of their expertise to the task.

Graciela explains that the team all visited sites where original paintwork from the period survives, studying the methods and the materials. 'We studied the original work with our conservationist eyes to determine how it was done and then carried it out, on site, with our fine art perspective,' she explains.

Visiting sites such as Winchester to view the 16th-century ceiling there was a real thrill. Plans inspired by it were then drawn for the new ceiling for the Queen's Inner Hall, sketches worked up to full-size drawings and finally, on a ground prepared by John Nevin and his team, Graciela's painters created their interpretation.

Graciela is particularly pleased with the effects in the Queen's Bedchamber, and few people will disagree when she enthuses, 'I'm not usually a fan of green. But this is beautiful! Beautiful! The richness is wonderful, a richness that comes from the best-quality pigments.'

In painting the Stirling Heads, her team were able to draw on their experience of carving and sculpture restoration. 'We were given broad guidance on colours but had to respect the carving,' she says. 'It's easy for paint to make a three-dimensional surface look flat; we had to use shading and colour to bring the carving out.'

CEILINGS

Finally, to the ceilings. These were a much more prominent part of high-status rooms in the 1500s than is usual today. Even where the ceiling was simply the underside of the rafters and floor-boards of the level above (as was often the case, even in high-status houses) it might be highlighted by elaborate painting. A more sophisticated idea, increasingly fashionable from the early 1500s, was to form a series of recessed (usually rectangular) cells framed by the beams running along and across the ceiling, now known as coffered ceilings. There are many ways of decorating them. All the evidence is that the Stirling Heads were originally mounted in just such a ceiling, and other Scots examples, more or less contemporary, are known from Kinneil, Holyrood and the chapel of Falkland Palace.

The Stirling Heads in the King's Inner Hall are considered in Chapter 7. In the Outer Halls, just the ribs of the coffers have been painted and the cells themselves left plain. In the Queen's Inner Hall both the frieze and the painted heads on the ceiling are derived from the nearly-contemporary work at Winchester College (now in the town's Westgate museum) with the addition of two heads based on portraits of James V and Mary of Guise. There is a clear parallel with the Stirling Heads and yet the effect is startlingly different.

In the bedchambers, the painted decoration within the coffers is heraldic, with monograms and antique work. At the intersections of the ribs there are bosses with further heraldic motifs appropriate to James V and Mary of Guise, both individually and as a couple, a format for which there are several examples, such as at Blois (France) and Losely Park (England).

Throughout the apartments, our attention flits from detail to overall effect. And at both levels the extravagant richness is obvious. There was no technical reason why the rooms might not have been made more convenient or more comfortable, though that would probably have involved sacrificing something of the spectacle. It is a sacrifice which few would want to make today, but which was essential for 16th-century monarchs, for whom a display of splendour was also a display of power and right.

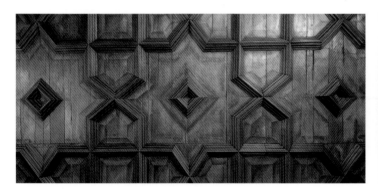

Above: A coffered ceiling at Kinneil House, near Bo'ness, between Stirling and Edinburgh.

Above: Two panels of a painted ceiling from Winchester College, which informed the ceiling of the Queen's Inner Hall.

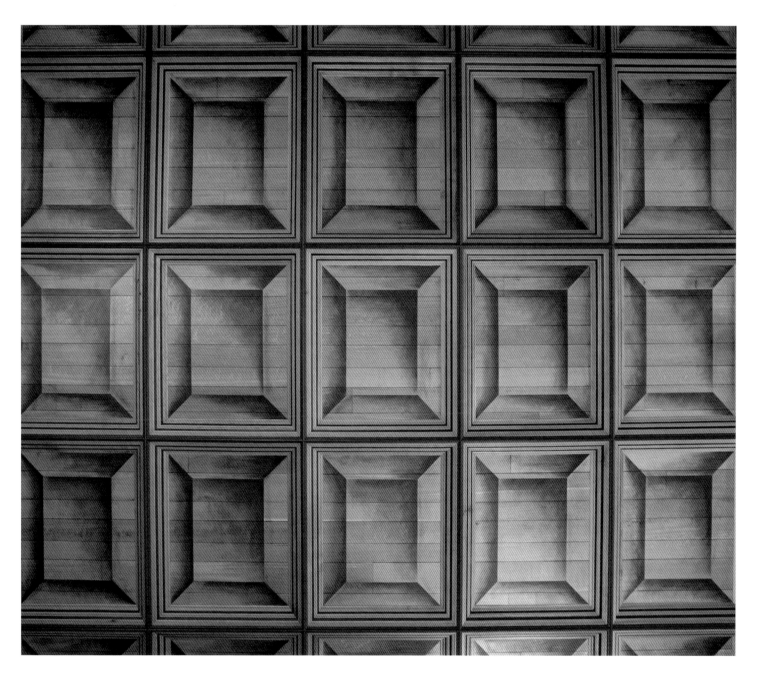

Above: The coffered ceiling of the Queen's Outer Hall.

5 COSTUME AND JEWELLERY
A COURTLY DRESS CODE

In the 1500s, the finest clothes of Europe's elite reached a degree of magnificence which has probably never been equalled. Costume was one of the ways in which James V sought to impress those around him, to stand out from the crowd, even to outshine the fabrics and furnishings of his own residences. Though monarchs had some more practical dress for riding, sports and so on, many of the clothes were wildly impractical.

Like jewellery, clothing was used by European monarchs as display and to convey messages about government and power, about dynasty and nation. Appropriate dress was an essential and direct expression of royal status. Even if the courtiers and attendants wore less lavish clothes, they were still far better dressed than the majority.

Left: A portrait of James V around 1540, resplendent in a gold and red gown sewn with thousands of pearls. He wears a heavy gold collar, embellished with thistles and hung with a pendant incorporating the saltire cross of St Andrew, patron saint of Scotland.

STYLE AT A PRICE

Records show that, in December 1538, livery-uniforms and other clothes were supplied for many members of the court and household. Those for the lowliest servants, the lads who turned spits in the kitchens, cost a modest £1.33 Scots. These boys were paid very little else, although they did get free board and lodging. Even the simplest of clothes were expensive: the materials were natural, the fabrics spun, woven and sewn by hand. As we move up the social hierarchy of the court, the liveries cost far more; around £10 for junior administrators and £50 each for the two master-households. In the same month, the queen's senior female attendants got new gowns and kirtles (outer petticoats) costing just over £88 for each outfit; while two chamber women got gowns of Paris black, lined with velvet, at a cost of £17 each.

Supplying these clothes, year by year, to a very large number of people was a significant cost. However, it was inescapable if the king and queen were to be attended by people who could adequately uphold the royal dignity. And, at first glance, the costs of many of the clothes for the king himself do not appear particularly high. That same month of December 1538, a new doublet for the king was lined, elaborately trimmed and fitted with gold buttons for £19.45; two pairs of hose for him cost £15.40, with a little extra for trimmings.

Still, the wild extravagance of the most ostentatious clothing is obvious. Two coats, both lined with cloth of gold and with gold fringes together cost £230; these must have been for Christmas and New Year as they so far outshone more routine supplies.

Most of our detailed information is from the period after the king's marriage trip to France in 1536. Contemporaries comment (some very critically) on the introduction of new and more extravagant fashions at court after the visit, so we would expect something more sombre for the earlier period. Certainly, for the later part of James V's reign and into the 1550s, the typical clothes for both men and women were those of the European mainstream. The king wore doublet and hose, the queen wore gown and kirtle. Distinctively Scots items are rare, but Highland tartan was supplied to make hose for the king in 1538 and a few other tartan items are mentioned, including two tartan 'galcolts' (a form of coat or jacket). Scottishness was more often reflected in trimmings such as gold buttons or 'horns' in the form of thistles. A few records of specific 'foreign' fashions creep in, such as the king's five 'Spanish' cloaks and a gown in the French style. These were probably widely worn in other countries, too, but it might be a nice compliment to wear a Spanish cloak when meeting a Spanish ambassador.

Above: A painting attributed to Corneille de Lyon, a painter at the French court. It has been identified as the noblewoman Gabrielle de Rochechouart. She wears a French hood and a 'triangular' narrow-waisted bodice with low square-cut neck. The puffy slashed sleeves are more typical of Italian and Spanish styles. All of these styles were adopted at the Scottish court.

Above: A painting by the 16th-century Venetian artist Titian. Known as *La Bella* ('The Beautiful Woman') it is thought to depict Eleanora de Gonzaga, Duchess of Urbino. In the Italian style, her sleeves are very full at the shoulder, while the slashed undersleeves are narrow from elbow to wrist. The low neckline and fuller waistline are also typically Italian. Again, these styles were very fashionable in Scotland.

HENRICVS II FRÃC̄   REX XR̃I
ANNO ÆTATIS SVÆ   XXXXVI

So, while few other men about the court were likely to wear cloth of gold, the king's routine dress was not so different from those of the men around him – indeed, he sometimes gave his cast-offs to courtiers, and the Regent Arran was wearing clothes from the royal wardrobe within days of the king's death. But the extent, richness and variety of the trimmings on the king's clothes were distinctive, as was the sheer number of items.

Trimmings were hugely important and ranged from expensive furs (ocelot, lynx, ermine, sable) to elaborate embroidery and gems and other jewellery items applied to the clothes. Many clothes were designed to show a lining in a different material from the face or were 'slashed' to show the under-fabric. Buttons and other closures were often of gold and even these might be further ornamented with enamels. A coat of black velvet was lined with taffeta and had 12 gold buttons, enamelled red and green. Each sleeve had six triangular gold buttons, enamelled in black. A riding cloak of purple velvet was bordered with gold crowns and probably had the king's monogram also in gold. Surely the most stunning of all, in 1539 the king had a robe and cape of cloth of gold, lined with crimson satin and trimmed with no fewer than 49,500 Orient pearls – even the gold buttons had their own settings of pearls.

Left: A portrait of King Henry II of France, who reigned 1547–59. He had close ties with the Scottish court: at different times, he was James V's brother-in-law and Mary Queen of Scots' father-in-law. In this painting of 1555, he wears a white doublet, a splendid black cape with white fur lining, a soft black hat with white plume and a heavy collar of gold and pearls with a gold pendant.

And the king's wardrobe was vast. The servant's livery often had to last all year. But in December 1538 alone, the king was supplied with at least eight pairs of hose, eight doublets and two gowns as well as the two fabulous coats. A wardrobe inventory at the time of his death lists 22 gowns, around 40 coats, five cloaks, over 50 doublets and 32 pairs of hose. The quality varied, and some, such as the six cloth coats, seem to have been for hunting, but a pair of red velvet breeks (trousers) is listed among sporting equipment, so the king was lavishly dressed even for hunting. With so many clothes, the king could change them frequently, appearing in several different outfits in one day. And variety was further expanded since sleeves, linings and trimmings were all regularly changed so that last week's doublet or cloak could look radically different next time it appeared. That was done 'in house' by members of the king's own household, which included specialist tailors, shoemakers, furriers, tapestry-repairers and others.

The king was supplied with several pairs of shoes in most months, and when he died he had around 40 pairs. While he was sometimes supplied with heavier footwear, many shoes were made of silk, velvet and similar materials – closer to slippers than to riding boots or heavy shoes for outdoor wear. This may have been a concession to the use of delicate and very expensive carpets on parts of the flooring.

Above: A portrait by Corneille de Lyon, usually identified as James V, though the figure bears scant resemblance to other portraits. He wears a high-necked black doublet, slashed to show a contrasting red lining, and a soft black hat with white plume. He has short hair, which became fashionable in the 1530s.

HEADWEAR

Men and women usually had their heads covered – both indoors and out. James V had a great many bonnets, often worn with elaborate 'targets', a type of badge or brooch, probably pinned to the bonnet. Some targets were gold or silver and studded with diamonds, one in the form of a mermaid set with diamonds, rubies and a great emerald. He had fewer hats and they tended to be plainer, five of black velvet and nine of silk. Like his ancestors, James V seems to have had long hair as a youth, adopting a fashionable shorter style by the later years of his reign. This is seen in Stirling Head 12, where his haircut is very like that of Francis I of France, but James is wearing a caul, a sort of fine skull-cap of gold thread, over his hair and under his bonnet, which was fashionable at the contemporary French court.

THE KING'S LIKENESS IN SILVER AND GOLD

Although Scots monarchs were more often seen by ordinary people than many of their contemporaries in England and the Continent, many Scots saw the king only on the coinage. So, coins allowed monarchs to create and to vary their image. This silver groat, of a style first minted in the 1520s, shows James V with the same long hair his ancestors had worn on their coins for generations.

The gold 'bonnet piece' dated 1540 (a more valuable coin) is much more modern in design, influenced by contemporary medal designs – and it shows him with newly-fashionable short hair.

Above: A portrait of James IV wearing a target on his bonnet.

JAMES IV – A ROYAL PENITENT

Magnificence and richness are our usual mental pictures of 16th-century royal dress. Expensive fabrics and furs, trimmed with gold and jewellery, indicate not just wealth but power and prestige – and that message is as easily read now as it was by observers of the time.

But who does this Stirling Head represent as he looks down at us from the ceiling of the King's Inner Hall? He certainly has a commanding gaze. But his dress is plain and unornamented – little more than a simple, loose-fitting gown.

Research for the Palace Project suggests that he is none other than James IV, king of Scotland and father of James V. Wouldn't the son have shown his father, a figure of European stature, as a more splendid and imposing figure than this? Indeed, many of the Heads are clearly based on portraits and depict their subjects wearing a wide range of rich and fashionable contemporary costumes.

In reality, he had good reason not to do so. As a youth, James IV had been implicated in an armed rising against his father, James III, who was defeated at the Battle of Sauchieburn (near Stirling) in 1488 and subsequently murdered. So, the new king was patently guilty of rebellion and of a role in the murder of his own father.

'He has a great predilection for priests, and receives advice from them, especially from the Friars Observant, with whom he confesses.'

Don Pedro de Alaya, Spanish ambassador at the court of James IV, around 1497

Treason and patricide were serious crimes. They violated treasured codes of honour and were sins of the first magnitude. Only the most onerous penitence and penance could wash away such a stain and validate the young man's claim to inherit his father's throne.

And, indeed, throughout the remainder of his life, James IV did penance, reputedly wearing a heavy chain round his waist, going on pilgrimages, fasting, and endowing Masses for his father's soul. Few kings can have so publicly aired their own awareness of the defects of their claim to kingship.

And if James IV's penance was not sufficient to validate his claim to the crown, then James V's claim as his son was also open to question. So here, perhaps, the long-dead James IV continues to wear his penitential gown – and so to endorse the royal rights of his son.

Women's head-dresses were more varied – as can be seen from the diversity of forms displayed on the Stirling Heads. They are sometimes described as 'English' or 'Spanish', but Italian and Spanish styles were widely worn in France and probably most of these 'national' styles were widely distributed.

It is the surviving accounts and wardrobe inventories which give us such a vivid view of the king's clothes. The separate records for the queen (whose finances were surprisingly independent of the king) do not survive, so we know much less about her clothes. However, again, she clearly dressed in broadly 'European' clothes. An exceptional payment for items supplied from the king's wardrobe for Christmas of 1539 includes some silver thread for sewing, some green velvet and some other quite minor items. But she was also given 15 ells of purple Venetian satin to make a gown. In December 1540 she was sent black Lucca velvet to make a gown, and crimson Venetian satin for a kirtle, so she was not going to be left in the shade that Christmas, anyway. The portraits differ markedly, with the best-known showing her in very sombre black and white and the most lavish in a stunning gown with remarkable jewellery. In general, however, the queen and her attendants were probably more sombrely dressed than the king.

Above: A portrait of a young woman, attributed to Hans Holbein the Younger and dated to the 1540s. At this time, Holbein was King's Painter at the Tudor court, so the subject is likely to be English, but she wears a French hood and a low, square-cut neckline, both of which were fashionable at the Scottish court. Her bulky, open-seamed sleeves are of a Spanish style also popular in Scotland.

COLOURS OF ROYALTY

Gold thread and purple and red dyes had been highly valued since antiquity due to their intrinsically high prices. In consequence they were seen as 'royal' colours and James V favoured them for important occasions. Other colours also had symbolic meanings and were thought appropriate to particular times or occasions – most obviously, both king and queen wore black mourning after the deaths of their two sons and the queen and her household again went into mourning after the death of the king. So clothes were probably stored by colour and this is, surely, why some of the wardrobe inventories list items by colour (purple doublets, white coats, black hose). But these listings also make clear that, however gorgeous the most extravagant clothes, there were also a great many black items, particularly for the more practical outer wear. Black was an expensive colour, not least as it was difficult to dye cloth black successfully, so it was very fashionable and Mary of Guise's attendants wore largely black liveries.

Ostentation, of course, has its drawbacks. Wearing a cloth of gold doublet, white hose, silk shoes and a bonnet decorated with substantial feathers virtually precluded any sort of outdoor activity and would even have been awkward for indoor dancing. Women's clothes were probably even more restricting as the bodices were stiffened with whalebone and tightened with lacing. Assistance with dressing and undressing was essential, not least as full-length mirrors were not available to ensure that hems were straight and pleats in place.

Above: A portrait of King Edward VI of England, around 1550, attributed to William Scrots, King's Painter at the English court. The son and successor of Henry VIII, Edward became king aged nine, and was about 12 when this portrait was made. He wears a black outfit, lavishly decorated with gold, which of course declares his wealth and power.

GOLD AND GEMSTONES

Some of the most ostentatious items were made of cloth of gold or trimmed with gold, precious stones, semi-precious stones and pearls. These are sometimes listed in the inventories along with the jewellery. A poignard (a small dagger) amongst the jewellery looks a little strange till we read that it was made of gold and agate, garnished with emeralds, rubies, diamonds and sapphires and was in a gold and silver scabbard. A chess set belonging to the king – the board of silver gilt and the men made of crystal and jasper – was sufficiently valuable to be listed with the crown, the sceptre and the other royal regalia. And James V had several heavy gold chains, on which he could hang his orders of chivalry or other badges. Much heavier than necklaces, they lay on the shoulders and fell to the breast.

He also had at least 31 'finger rings', some with diamonds and other gem stones – in one portrait (see page 82) he wears such a ring on his right forefinger – and a good many loose diamonds, other gems and pearls. Mary of Guise had some gems as queen consort of Scotland but would also have had jewellery of her own, brought from France. In the double portrait now displayed at Blair Castle (see page 36) she has some huge rubies on the breast of her gown and in the Hardwick Hall portrait (see page 16) she wears a four-stranded necklace.

Above: Holbein's portrait of Jane Seymour, third wife of Henry VIII. She wears a distinctive, angular English hood. Her dress's 'trumpet' sleeves, narrow waist and square neckline are all French styles that were also popular in Scotland. She wears gems, pearls and gold in abundance. The centrepiece features the letters IHS, for 'Jesus'. It is listed in an inventory of the time, which notes it includes 23 diamonds, three emeralds, a ruby and three pearls.

THE SIGNIFICANCE OF GIFTS

Important though the clothes and jewellery were as aspects of royal display, they were also crucial to a complex system of gifts and exchange which operated in and around all royal courts. Just as the king and queen gave and received gifts of horses, hawks and other valuable items, so they gave and received items of jewellery and gave cloth and items of clothing. Francis I had given James V a 'whinger' (a short sword) in a golden sheath, both set with precious stones. James's stepson Francis (the only surviving child of Mary of Guise's first marriage) gave him a gold ornament or brooch. The king gave numerous presents of cloth and clothes of varying qualities. In March 1539, he ordered £400 in a purse decorated with gold as a present to a messenger sent from the king of France. Royal gifts were highly prized and a century later, in 1640, the lairds of Glenorchy still treasured a target of gold, set with diamonds, topazes, a ruby and a sapphire, given to an earlier laird by James V. Seen in that light, jewellery and fine clothes were not a bad long-term investment, reaping a return of loyalty and dynastic attachment. But gifts had to be appropriate to giver and recipient. And while other people might be happy to receive the royal cast-offs, the king's and queen's clothes were always newly made!

Above: Scotland's Sword of State and its elaborately decorated scabbard. Created by the Italian cutler Domenico da Sutri, they were presented to James IV by Pope Julius II in 1507. This was an invaluable token of papal favour, which prompted a letter of gratitude from James. As one element of the Honours of Scotland (crown jewels), the sword was used at coronations thereafter. The Honours are now displayed at Edinburgh Castle.

LIVE INTERPRETATION AND COSTUMES: BOB AND HILARY HOLSMAN

However important the architecture, the furniture or the other physical aspects of the Palace, the court was about people. Bringing back that human dimension is the responsibility of Bob and Hilary Holsman and their team.

Costumed interpreters at Stirling present a range of documented characters from the 1540s – from domestic servants to courtiers. Members of this team are now always present in the Palace interiors to welcome visitors.

Dressing the interpreters has involved becoming intimately familiar with some surprisingly obscure issues. Hilary explains how a Scotswoman of the 1540s would have put on a simple head-dress, folding the linen and tucking, tying and pinning it over her braided hair, forming a complex but neatly-ordered head-covering. And doing this without a thought. But that takes practice and it is a trick the female interpreters have had to acquire. 'Nor can you get away from the issue of the weight of the clothes,' Hilary says. 'They were lined and padded and stiffened. They are very difficult indeed in warm weather – to say nothing of the issues of long hems wearing on stone floors or trailing on wet surfaces.'

Bob emphasises that having the team ready has involved a lot of detailed and eclectic study. 'We have looked at topics from the daily routine, to how to manage a coal fire, from how a person's status would affect their deportment, to how and why servants might "misbehave". The aim is that the interpreters can present the information that the astonishing range of visitors would want, in a pleasant and accessible manner. Like putting on that head-dress, it needs to be second nature.'

Above: Bob and Hilary Holsman at work on outfits for the costumed interpreters.

THE ROYAL WARDROBE

For James V and Mary of Guise, getting dressed was a complicated business which would certainly have involved servants. Their clothes were designed for show more than comfort, and would often have been changed more than once a day. These illustrations show the layers of garments that made up a royal outfit.

The king's underwear is a long silk shirt which he tucks between his legs.

On his legs he wears wool or silk stockings, held up with garters.

Next comes a pair of trunk hose with a separate codpiece covering his groin.

He adds a padded doublet, fashionably slashed to show the lining fabric.

Next he puts on a jerkin, a sleeveless coat with knee-length skirt.

A velvet bonnet and luxurious fur-lined gown complete the ensemble.

The queen's underwear is
a long smock made from silk.

On her upper body she wears a tight
corset with a stiff, flat front.

Next comes a petticoat with wooden
hoops called a Spanish farthingale.

Over this she wears a kirtle (a full underskirt).
Separate sleeves are pinned on.

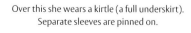

Her floor-length gown is worn
with an open skirt at the front.

Finally, she wears a French hood and
plenty of jewellery, including a girdle belt.

PALACE FASHION

We now know a lot about what people wore at Stirling in the 1540s. On pages 98–103, costumed interpreters model some of the clothes created for use in live presentations at the Palace.

Top: A young lady of the court wears a French hood and a gown of black velvet. The sleeves are slashed with red satin, and the linen cuffs are finely embroidered with black work.

Above: Two maids of the court wear functional wool and white linen. The mistress of the laundry wears a satin gown and French hood.

Top: A liveried servant wears a suit of French black wool. His red wool bonnet marks him out as a servant of the Scottish royal court.

Above: A low-status servant wears clothing made from undyed wool, and a caul (or cap) of plain linen. His bonnet has been felted by brushing with heads of teasel, a barbed wildflower.

This page: The queen wears a gown of silk damask in royal purple, with trumpet sleeves trimmed in white fur. Her kirtle, or underskirt, is made from Italian silk cloth, encrusted with over 600 'Scotch' pearls. On her breast she wears a brooch inspired by the one worn by Jane Seymour in Holbein's portrait (see page 93).

Above: The queen (left) and her ladies wear
their hair tied back, identifying them as married
women. All three wear fashionable French hoods.

Above: The queen's upper body would be very restricted by the boned corset she wears under her gown and kirtle. Her jewellery includes a five-stranded pearl necklace and a large emerald set in a gold ring.

Above: A gentleman of the court wears a silk brocade doublet with gilt pomegranate buttons and a black velvet bonnet adorned with a crane's feather. He wears four finger-rings set with gemstones and a pearl ear-ring in his ear, which is pierced in the French manner.

Above: The queen's master of the hunt wears Stewart royal livery
of red and gold. His clothes are made of wool, functional and warm.
The dogs are fast, intelligent Scottish deerhounds, which were used
for hunting in 16th-century Scotland, in packs of up to 16.

Above: These two young courtiers sport European fashions. The gentleman on the left wears a French suit of tanny velvet with Turkish gold braid, trimmed with fur. His companion wears a black suit influenced by Italian styles. His trunk hose features a prominent white codpiece, known in Scotland as a pouch.

Above: A herald (left) wears a taffeta tabard in Scottish royal livery. The lion rampant is painted rather than embroidered, marking him out as a royal pursuivant. His livery would be gifted annually as part of his pay. The French 'warman' (right) is dressed to emulate his king, Francis I. He wears black doublet with gold braid, black gown trimmed with fur and a black steel helmet with black plume.

6 THE UNICORN TAPESTRIES
WEAVING STORIES

Tapestries were among the most luxurious possessions of elite households in the 1500s. Even the plainest wall-hangings were prestigious, mitigating the harshness of bare walls and perhaps retaining some of the heat. But the most elaborate were vastly expensive works of art, depicting complex scenes and conveying sophisticated intellectual ideas, as well as being expressions of their owners' wealth and taste.

The cost of tapestries was prodigious and a full set could cost as much as a warship. Few can ever have rivalled the *Hunt of the Unicorn* set now housed in the Cloisters Museum for Medieval Art and Architecture, part of the Metropolitan Museum in New York. A new set of tapestries, closely modelled on these stunning hangings, is being woven to display in the Queen's Inner Hall at Stirling.

Left: The central figure of the unicorn, as depicted in the final tapestry of the set, 'The Unicorn in Captivity'.

A ROYAL TAPESTRY COLLECTION

James V had around 200 hangings and tapestries, in a number of series. Several tapestry sets were bought while he was in France on his wedding trip, or shortly thereafter. Tapestries were very suitable for a mobile court as they could be readily moved and re-hung as required – though that inevitably involved some damage, one of the reasons why so few survive. James V's collection included stories from the Bible and from Classical antiquity, as well as hunting scenes and two sets called *The Great Unicorn* and *The Little Unicorn*, comprising six and eight tapestries respectively. The last record of them refers to four surviving pieces in 1578. However, sets or part sets of unicorn tapestries do survive elsewhere, including the tapestries from the Cloisters. The hunts depicted are very similar to realistic contemporary stag hunt tapestries, but these unicorns are allegorical, mystical and even (as we shall see) divine.

Images and stories of unicorns go back for well over 2,000 years. They were thought to live in exotic places – perhaps in deep forests 'far, far away' – and to have mysterious properties. Even people who thought they were real animals did not think that they were ordinary animals. The horn of the unicorn, in particular, was imbued with mystical and perhaps miraculous powers and 'unicorn horns' were prized possessions. James IV had one set in gold – in reality probably an Arctic narwhal horn – mounted as a cup to protect against poisoning.

Scots had been familiar with heraldic unicorns as supporters of the royal arms of Scotland since the early 1400s. In this setting the unicorns were chained, the implication being that these famously haughty and even fierce creatures had been tamed and brought into royal service. James V had a golden cup decorated with a unicorn and his own arms on the cover; his two royal barges were *The Lion* and *The Unicorn*. There was even a Scots gold coin known as a unicorn, with a unicorn on the obverse.

THE CLOISTERS TAPESTRIES

The tapestries in New York can be dated to about 1500 by details such as dress and shoe styles. Like many of the finest tapestries, they were woven in the southern Netherlands. Such superlative tapestries as these were always woven to order. There are now six substantially intact tapestries and two fragments of a seventh, though other pieces may have been lost. Like other fine tapestries, these were for display in the inner and most prestigious parts of a residence. The recurring use of the monogram 'AE' (with the E reversed) suggests that all seven must have belonged to the same family, though their history before the later 1600s is unknown. There have been several different views as to how the seven pieces relate to each other. In any case, ambiguity and multiple interpretations were probably a part of the original plan. These were never intended to be works to grasp at a glance. The viewer was expected to study the layers of meaning and work at them, as well as marvel at them. With those qualifications, it does seem clear that the central message of six of the tapestries is a religious allegory.

Above: A narwhal horn from the collection of maritime artefacts at Trinity House in Leith, Edinburgh. For centuries, narwhal horns were sold as unicorn horns.

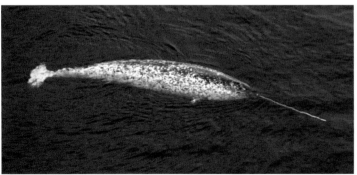

Top: A tapestry produced around 1510 shows the Annunciation, the moment when the Virgin Mary learns she is pregnant. James V's tapestry collection included biblical scenes similar to this.

Above: A narwhal in its Arctic habitat.

Top: A tapestry from the series *The Lady with the Unicorn*, produced in the 1480s and now held at Museum of Cluny in Paris.

Above: The initials 'AE' as they appear on the original tapestries.

THE SCOTTISH UNICORN

In stories about unicorns, they usually had to be tamed before they could be captured or controlled. That is symbolised in the royal arms of Scotland, as the chained unicorns support the crowned central shield, representing the monarchy. There is a clear similarity with the final tapestry, where the tamed unicorn sits, chained to the tree in the garden, an image which has sometimes been seen as a symbol of marriage.

Heraldic unicorns are common motifs on Scots market crosses and appear on heraldic panels, inside and outside contemporary buildings.

Since early Christian times, it had been thought that the powerful unicorn could only be tamed by a virgin (a personification of innocence). Like stags, unicorns came to be compared to Christ. A bestiary of the 1100s claimed that stags would draw venomous serpents from pools and kill them with their feet, just as Christ triumphed over sin. Mary of Guise would have known the 22 mural paintings at her uncle's residence at Nancy (France), which compared the life of Christ with the life of a stag and ended with the stag being hunted and killed. James V had a set of bed hangings which compared the life of man to the life of a stag. In the murals at Nancy, the hunting of the stag began at the moment when Judas betrayed Christ, when the pursuit by his enemies entered its final phase, leading inexorably to his death. The capture of the unicorn or stag became a metaphor for Christ entering the Virgin's womb (the Incarnation); this was the essential preliminary for his birth and so for human redemption from sin.

Above: The royal arms of Scotland with unicorn supporters in a colourful rendition at Edinburgh Castle.

Above: A prayer to the Virgin Mary inscribed on a huntsman's scabbard.

THE MEANING OF THE HUNT

The sequence of tapestries (shown in full on pages 115–21) can be read as a 'story'. In the first tapestry, 'The Start of the Hunt', the huntsmen gather for the start of the hunt, and the scout among the trees directs them to the unseen quarry. In the second, 'The Unicorn is Found', a man at the extreme left, pointing to the unicorn with a very shifty expression, represents Judas at the moment he betrays Christ. The hunters have found their quarry but their animated expressions suggest that they realise this is no ordinary beast. The unicorn dips its horn into the serpent-poisoned water, to purify it so that the other animals (who surround the fountain) can drink.

In the next piece, 'The Unicorn Leaps out of the Stream', the hunted unicorn has plunged into a stream, to cool itself and elude pursuit. But it already has blood trickling from its rump. In the fourth piece, 'The Unicorn at Bay', the unicorn resists a ferocious attack by bucking and kicking; it has gored one of the hounds. The hunter with a horn may represent the Angel Gabriel; his scabbard is inscribed with a prayer to the Virgin Mary. The final stages of the hunt are represented in the sixth tapestry, 'The Unicorn is Killed and Brought to the Castle'. In the left background, the assistant hunters hold the unicorn at bay while the master of the hunt moves in to

give the final thrust with his sword; in the foreground the dead unicorn is slung across the back of a horse, just as a dead stag would be. So the death of the unicorn represents the Passion – the suffering and death of Jesus Christ.

In a real stag hunt the quarry would now be carried back in triumph to the castle (which has appeared in the background of the previous hangings). However, the faces of those who emerge from the castle to the back right do not suggest rejoicing – rather, they are torn by profound grief, and the leading woman is holding her rosary, as though at prayer (see page 126). Unlike the hunters, with their often-cruel features and sullen expressions, these people recognise the enormity of the death and they probably represent those who were present when Christ was taken down from the Cross. But they know, too, that this death will bring human redemption.

Of course, the death of Christ is not the end of the story. Rather, in the final hanging of the series, the unicorn is alive again, enclosed within a pen or garden, chained to a tree, clearly suggesting the Resurrection.

WEAVING THE NEW TAPESTRIES

The new tapestries differ in some ways from the old. Not least, they will compensate for some of the damage to the originals over the last 500 years. The new yarns will heighten the colour palette. And although the wool and the gold thread will be very similar to the original, mercerised cotton has been used in place of silk, since it is much more durable and will give a very similar effect. The new tapestries are about 10 per cent smaller, to fit the spaces available. The initials 'AE' which appear on the originals (with the E reversed) are not being included.

The two fragments of 'The Mystic Hunt' present a huge challenge. Though the huntsman is complete, his hounds and the unicorn are not. The figure of Eve is nearly complete but only part of a hand (resting on the unicorn's mane) survives of another figure, that of the Maiden. New areas will be designed and woven so that the two fragments once again form a single piece.

The work has been undertaken by an international team from the West Dean Tapestry Studio (Sussex, England). Some of the work, including design, weaving, finishing and management, has been carried out at West Dean. Meanwhile, much of the weaving has been executed in a specially constructed building at Stirling, where the public have been able to watch its slow progress. The whole project will have taken 12 years by the time the last tapestry is finished in 2013.

The total cost of the tapestry project is around £2 million, funded separately from the main Palace Project. The principal sponsor has been the Quinque Foundation of the United States, with further support from the Guild of Weavers and donations from the public. The co-operation of the Metropolitan Museum of Art in New York has also been crucial; in addition to granting permission for the copies to be woven, they have allowed the weavers privileged private access to the original tapestries, essential for the research.

Above: Weavers at work on one of the new tapestries in the Stirling studio.

MILLEFLEURS AND MYSTERIES

The first and last of this series are woven in a distinctive style known as *millefleurs* ('thousand flowers') from the floral background. James V's *Great Unicorn* series may have been something like this, a theme sometimes called 'The Hunt of the Unicorn as an Allegory of the Passion'.

The two fragments of the remaining tapestry, 'The Mystic Hunt of the Unicorn', comprise a substantial part of a single hanging – and the new tapestry has been designed as a single 'complete' piece. It would have hung alone and its 'story' does not directly relate to the others. Eve stands on the left, under an apple tree, with a sly sidelong glance. A woman's hand rests on the unicorn's neck though the rest of her body is missing; she is the Maiden who will subdue the unicorn. Now, at the sounding of the hunter's horn, the unicorn (Christ) will enter the fenced garden, which symbolises the Incarnation.

The tapestries copied for the project are distinguished by the extraordinary skill in the depiction of plants, the subtlety and variety of the facial expressions and the astonishing realism of rich fabrics such as velvet. The colours, too, are amazingly bright. But the newly created pieces are even more vivid than the 500-year-old source material. Part of the excitement of seeing something so wonderful in its new state is to realise that these new tapestries will also still be beautiful and admired in another 500 years' time.

Top: A tapestry known as *Le Chevalier*, woven near Calais in the late 1400s. Its background is a splendid example of *millefleurs*.

Above left: A *millefleurs* detail from 'The Start of the Hunt'.

Above right: Another *millefleurs* detail, from 'The Unicorn in Captivity'.

TAPESTRIES: CARRON PENNEY

Carron Penney has led the tapestry project for West Dean Tapestry Studio since the start of the weaving project in 2001, and the last piece will not be hung till 2013. 'A huge part of my life,' she acknowledges. It's been a learning experience for her and for her teams at West Dean and Stirling, who continue to work with contemporary artists interpreting modern paintings. But in this case, too, she emphasises, they are first and foremost artist weavers re-interpreting the work.

'It's difficult to make parallels with the original work,' she says. 'We use many of the same materials but the weavers were trained in a different way. They were generally younger than most weavers today and could work only in daylight; there might have been five or six people working at one loom, very close together.' Working in a well-lit, warm site at Stirling, watched by the public, is very different. 'This is an opportunity to represent tapestry that could not have been better and has brought it to a huge audience,' she emphasises.

Weaving 'medieval' tapestries is a new experience for many of the team. 'The work is much finer and uses techniques such as hachures and demi-duite to give shading and three-dimensional effects, which are quite different from contemporary work. But people will see these tapestries on the walls, perhaps for generations to come; tapestry, as an art form, can only benefit from that.'

Top: Carron Penney (left) working with colleagues at West Dean

Above: At work on a detail for 'The Unicorn is Found'.

Above: A selection of coloured threads to be woven into a tapestry.

THE GREYHOUND – SPORTING DOG OF THE TUDORS

While most dogs were despised in the 1500s, hunting hounds were greatly valued for their faithfulness and loyalty as well as their hunting prowess. It is no coincidence that these were also among the good qualities of a 'noble' man. Greyhounds of various kinds, including deerhounds, were particularly prized, and Scots hunting hounds had an international reputation. James V often gave Scots hounds to foreign rulers.

Many of the dogs which appear in the unicorn tapestries are of the greyhound type. The greyhounds' task was to run the quarry down and exhaust it, ready for the master of the hunt to strike the fatal blow. They are depicted as vivacious, alert and attentive, their fine skin flowing over spare muscular bodies, with broad, ornamented collars which indicate who owned them. That is the sort of realistic detail which makes the tapestries so stunning, but it also suggests the pride that owners took in these prized animals.

This woman, wearing an English hood and holding a tiny greyhound, is thought to be Margaret Tudor, mother of James V and sister of Henry VIII of England. The greyhound was a badge of the Tudors and her presence among the Stirling Heads is a reminder that through her, as a grandson of Henry VII of England, James V had a claim to the English throne if Henry VIII and his line should fail.

Above: Stirling Head 17, which depicts James V's mother, Margaret Tudor. She holds a greyhound, which was a popular hunting dog of the time, and also a symbol of the Tudors.

Above: One of the many greyhounds which appear in the tapestries.

THE ORIGINAL TAPESTRIES

The seven tapestries commissioned for Stirling Castle Palace
are closely based on a set displayed at the Cloisters Museum
in New York. This set did not belong to James V, but it
was produced around the same time as his own Unicorn
tapestries, and probably in the same region of what was
then the Netherlands. The original tapestries are shown
on pages 115–21.

'And often times [the king] will buy
rich hangings and other apparel for
his houses … For if a king did not so,
nor might do, he lived then not like his
estate, but rather in misery, and in more
subjection than doth a private person.'

Sir John Fortescue,
The Governance of England, around 1450

Above: The original tapestry, 'The Start of the Hunt'.

Above: The original tapestry, 'The Unicorn is Found'.

Above: The original tapestry, 'The Unicorn Leaps out of the Stream'.

Above: The original tapestry, 'The Unicorn at Bay'.

Above: The two fragments of the original tapestry, 'The Mystic Hunt of the Unicorn'.

Above: The original tapestry, 'The Unicorn is Killed and Brought to the Castle'.

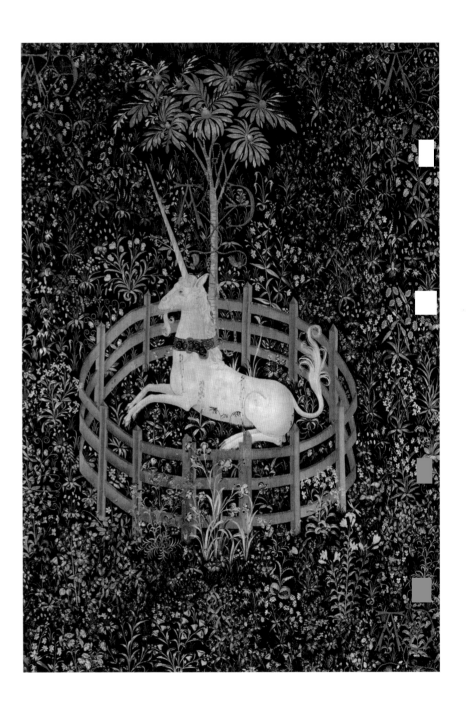

Above right: The original tapestry, 'The Unicorn in Captivity'.

THE NEW TAPESTRIES

Work began on the seven new tapestries in 2000. The last
is due for completion in 2013, with four woven in Stirling
and three at the team's permanent base at West Dean in
West Sussex. Four pieces were complete at the point when
the Palace was re-opened to the public, and are shown
on pages 122–9.

Above: A *millefleurs* detail from 'The Start of the Hunt'.
Among the flowers shown here are hawkweed and honesty.

Above: The scout summons the
huntsmen, having spotted the unicorn.

Above: Two dogs, possibly bloodhounds.

Above: The new tapestry, 'The Start of the Hunt'.

Above: The new tapestry, 'The Unicorn is Found'.

'And immediately, while he yet spake, cometh Judas, one of the twelve, and with him a great multitude with swords and staves, from the chief priests and the scribes and the elders. And he that betrayed him had given them a token, saying, 'Whomsoever I shall kiss, that same is he; take him, and lead him away safely.'

Mark 14:43–44

Top: The pointing figure at the left probably represents Judas, the disciple who betrayed Christ.

Above: A cringing wolf is one of the creatures waiting to drink water purified by the unicorn's horn.

Top: The figures emerging from the castle seem awed by the unicorn's death.

Above: An assistant hunter weakens the unicorn with a spear thrust.

Above: The master of the hunt with his sword, ready to deliver the *coup de grâce*, or fatal blow.

Above: The new tapestry, 'The Unicorn is Killed and Brought to the Castle'.

Above: The new tapestry, 'The Unicorn in Captivity'.

'Those who seek to
  Capture and tether [the unicorn] …
Must find a young woman
They know to be a virgin
Then have her sit and wait …
When the unicorn comes
And espies the maiden
It no sooner sees her
Than it prostrates itself before her
At which those lying in wait rush out.
They seize it and tie it up
And bring it before the king.'

Guillaume, Clerk of Normandy,
The Divine Bestiary, around 1210

Above: The tree to which the unicorn is
tethered bears pomegranates, whose red
juice represents Christ's blood.

Above: The white flower below
the unicorn's tail is Madonna lily,
symbolising the Virgin Mary.

7 THE STIRLING HEADS
PORTRAITS IN OAK

The group of carved oak roundels known as the Stirling Heads are among the finest artistic productions of 16th-century Scotland. Travellers who saw them in their original locations on the Palace ceilings highlighted their quality. But all the carved woodwork was stripped from the royal apartments in 1777 and, though some Heads were preserved, some were destroyed and the survivors were dispersed.

During the Palace Project, all the known surviving Heads were located and brought together. Most of these are now displayed, with other fragments, on the top floor of the Palace. The project has also commissioned a new series of Heads, which have been mounted in the ceiling of the King's Inner Hall, painted as the originals surely were, to form a major highlight of the recreated Royal Lodgings.

Left: Stirling Head 40, representing Mary of Guise.
The flowers in her hand signify her marriage to James V.

A UNIQUE SURVIVAL

The Stirling Heads are among the very few decorative features to survive from the 16th-century Palace, making them uniquely important. Carved of solid oak, they are surprisingly robust for their age, but replacing them in anything like their original locations would have involved unacceptable risk of damage to these priceless objects, while making further detailed study impossible. So, the decision to 'conserve and display' the originals was taken even before the Palace Project was under way. In fact, the high quality of the Heads had an important influence on the whole project, for they support the suggestion that the rest of the decoration, aspects which do not survive, would be of similar quality and similarly 'modern' for the early 1540s. For modern the Heads certainly were, as we shall see shortly.

There are 34 surviving Heads and some fragments; there are drawings of two more which were destroyed by fire in 1940; and there is evidence that there must once have been at least 45 Heads, perhaps more. The impetus of the Palace Project has made it possible to bring the survivors together for the first time in almost 250 years, including three in the collections of the National Museums Scotland. And this, in turn, has allowed detailed examination and comparison of all the Heads, as well as facilitating the carving of the new ones. A major academic study made an important breakthrough in suggested identities for many of the individual Heads. This made it possible to grasp James V's intention in creating such a splendid, unique and prodigiously expensive scheme.

The replica Heads, of which there are 37, have been painstakingly carved by hand, just as they would have been in the 1500s, and painted in accordance with the latest understanding.

Tree-ring analysis of several Heads revealed that most of the oak had grown in the area of modern Poland and was felled around 1539. Work was already under way on the Palace by that date, so little time can have been wasted in transporting, working and mounting. This suggests the hurry and bustle which surrounded the building work. John Donaldson, the carver of the replica Heads, has suggested that the boards may have been imported as barrel-staves, which might explain the variable dimensions of the Heads and some aspects of the carving, too. Together, these insights enliven and enrich our view of the creation of the whole Palace, not just the Heads.

Another aspect of the scientific examination was the search for traces of original paint. These were sparse and often faint, perhaps not surprisingly since by the 1800s the taste was for polished wood, so visible paint traces could have been regarded as 'dirt' to be removed. But, for the project team, searching for evidence of the Heads' original appearance, the smallest surviving fragments were vital clues, part of the evidence in this cultural detective story.

THE STIRLING HEADS IN POSITION

1 Male Worthy	**11** Roman emperor	**24** John, Duke of Albany	**34** Hercules with his club
2 Male Worthy	**12** James V	**25** Noblewoman	**36** Jester
3 Male Worthy	**13** Charles V	**26** Madeleine de Valois	**37** *Putto*
4 Male Worthy	**14** Poet	**27** James IV	**38** *Putto*
5 Hercules	**16** Noblewoman	**28** Noblewoman	**39** Henry VIII
6 Roman emperor	**17** Margaret Tudor	**29** Woman in masquing costume	**40** Mary of Guise
7 Julius Caesar	**18** Noblewoman	**30** Hercules	**41** Female Worthy
8 Emperor Titus	**20** Female Worthy	**31** Roman emperor	
9 James I	**22** Nobleman	**32** Roman emperor	
10 Male Worthy	**23** Nobleman	**33** Hercules slays a lion	

Numbering the Heads: The numbering system used to identify the Stirling Heads relates to their acquisition and was not used to inform the arrangement of the replica Heads on the ceiling.

The carvings numbered 15, 19, 21 and 35 survive only as fragments and are now recognised as likely to be from panelling. They are not shown here.

Above: The replica Stirling Heads in position on the ceiling of the King's Inner Hall.

KNOWN BY REPUTATION

The team were well aware of reports that, around 1800, some of the Heads were stored in the prison in Stirling, where the prisoners passed the time by painting them with whatever came to hand. But the prisoners were not likely to have access to indigo, for example. It is very expensive, and although it was widely used in the 1500s, it was obsolete by 1700! The most extensive traces were of white-lead oil paint, probably a ground-layer, with the other colours applied over it, a technique well-known in the 1500s. There were other paint traces, particularly related to the colour of clothes and a characteristic grey-blue found on armour and helmets, intended to give a metallic sheen. All these hints contributed towards creating a credible colour scheme for the new Heads, though other ideas were drawn from portraits, contemporary fashions and (for the 16th-century Scots) from wardrobe inventories and accounts which describe the colours of clothes (see Chapter 5).

The historical descriptions by visitors in the 1600s and 1700s all agreed on the quality of the work. The English naturalist John Ray, who visited about 1660, was one of the first to comment on the 'very good carved wood-work on the roofs' of the former Royal Lodgings. The gentleman traveller John Macky wrote in 1723 that there was nothing at Windsor or Hampton Court Palace to compare. But, like others, these visitors give only hazy and sometimes conflicting accounts of how many Heads there were and their precise locations. The balance of the evidence is that many were originally displayed in the King's Inner Hall, in a coffered ceiling of the kind now recreated in the other apartments (see Chapter 4). That is how the new painted Heads are mounted, ranged in groups, such as 'family members' and 'heroes of the ancient world', to which we shall turn shortly.

GETTING OUR HEADS EXAMINED

Head 29 is a female figure wearing a fantastical costume. This is now thought to be a masquing costume, an elaborate disguise used in courtly entertainments. Her open mouth might suggest that she is singing. She joins other evidence that the court of James V was familiar with Classical, allegorical forms of entertainment. Some of the other figures wear fashionable contemporary dress (including Italian and English styles); the dress of the 'historical' figures, however, is often very unrealistic, little more than guess-work.

But Head 10 was of particular interest, as traces of paint have been found on it, red on the lips and blue on the armour, evidence of the original colour-scheme.

Above: Head 29, showing a lady of the court in masquing costume.

Above: Traces of the original paint were found on Head 10, representing a male Worthy.

COMMISSIONING THE HEADS

Another set of puzzles focused on why James V would commission such a magnificent and hugely expensive ceiling – for it would have cost a vast sum. Apart from materials and workmanship, the commission would have required a phase of research and design, allowing appropriate source materials, such as printed illustrations, to be located. Some Heads are so detailed that they must derive from portraits, and there is some evidence that James V had portraits of some of his Scots ancestors and other relatives. The French portrait painter Pierre Quesnel was a member of Mary of Guise's household.

To answer the 'why?' question, we need to know a little more about the 'what?'. The Stirling Heads are what art historians call 'medallion heads'. These were originally inspired by coins and medals derived from ancient Roman models, in vogue from the 1400s. By the 1530s they were being created to adorn high-status buildings and tombs at a number of places across Europe, indoors and out, in media from paint to plaster and stone. The earliest known examples in Scotland are in stone at Falkland Palace, probably carved a few years before the Stirling Heads. In interiors, they were often wood, most frequently as panelling on walls or furniture (as, for example, the armoire in the Queen's Bedchamber – see page 66–7).

As the Renaissance advanced, the styles of medallion heads changed, abandoning the formal profile and dress of the originals. At Stirling we do not just have heads but busts and full-length figures. James V's medallions were not just 'in the fashion' but were at the forefront, with their stylish dress and their varied gestures and direction of gaze, from profile to full-face. These qualities did not become usual for another decade or so. Indeed, while the Stirling Heads have been compared to the carved heads at Wawel Castle (Cracow, Poland) and with work at Azay-le- Rideau (Indre-et-Loire, France) among others, the connections are tenuous. The Stirling Heads are unique in style. They use the circular format with its iconography of fame and immortality – the laurel or bay wreath – adapting it to other storylines to suit James V's specific agenda. They celebrate dynasty, a glittering court, international recognition, chivalry and humanist virtues.

So, the educated visitor, arriving in Stirling, saw something which was very unusual and astonishingly up-to-date. Such modishness was every bit as impressive as the luxurious fabrics and the 'grotesque' decoration. Creating an impression was certainly one of James V's major aims, and he was prepared to spend lavishly to achieve this.

Above: Two of the medallion heads carved in stone at Falkland Palace in Fife, one of James V's principal residences.

Above: One of the carved wooden heads at Wawel Castle in Poland.

IDENTIFYING THE SUBJECTS

Probably, like modern visitors, our educated 16th-century visitor, having finished gasping, would turn to the issue of identification. Some Heads would have been instantly recognisable – as some still are. But perhaps, even then, some could only be identified with help from people who knew what was intended. That would not have detracted from the message. Uncertainty made the Heads into conversation pieces, focused attention on them and reinforced the lessons. Today, with that original certainty lost, it has involved much detailed scholarly research to restore identities to a sufficient sample of the Heads to allow modern visitors to grasp the outline of the themes and so to bring us a step closer to James V's purposes. But it has to be emphasised that there are plenty of questions unanswered.

Sometimes the problem of identity is easily solved. But, as the case of the jester shows, even knowing who someone is does not necessarily resolve what the figure means (see page 19). And the task is complicated by a court culture which rejoiced in double and treble meanings.

In the 1700s and early 1800s, at least, there was a tradition that some of the Heads – but clearly not all – depicted kings and queens of Scotland. Some of the more specific identifications made then are probably wrong, but decorative schemes involving 'family galleries' in various media were very fashionable, and details of several of the Heads fit well with the appearance or biographies of members of James V's extended family. Of course, it has to be remembered that not all the original Heads survive, so we have to expect 'empty seats' at the family table.

Above: A painting of James I, great-great-grandfather of James V, who was king of Scots, 1406–37. The painting dates from the mid-1500s and may not be an accurate likeness.

Above: Original Head 9, representing James I.

Research for the Palace Project supports the traditional view that Head 12 represents James V himself. Though he has no specific identifying features, the Head does have the long, fine features and the formal pose of his portraits. Here he presents himself as the perfect prince of contemporary theory, noble and majestic, combining virtue with distinguished descent. The clothes are rather sketchily indicated but are clearly luxurious and contemporary, and giving them the Stewart dynastic colours of crimson and gold makes the identification a matter of course.

Research has identified two further Stewart kings, James IV (James V's father) and James I (James V's great-great-grandfather). The king's mother, Margaret Tudor, is also present (see page 113). Head 9 has traditionally been identified as James I, but this proved difficult to confirm. The surviving 'portraits' of James I (1394–1437) were not only painted long after the king's death but after the creation of the Stirling Heads, and the first identification of this Head (in *Lacunar Strevelinense*) was based on an engraving of the king published in 1602. But at least one of the portraits of him, though far too late to be the source for the Head, is so 'individual' that it is probably a copy of an authentic original.

It was a common practice to have ancestral and contemporary portraits copied – Mary of Guise sent just such a copy of a portrait of James V to her own mother, who much admired it. Mary Queen of Scots had a sequence of dynastic portraits which were listed after her execution. James I was certainly familiar with cultures where portraits were painted and circulated, and it is possible that his own portrait was painted during his lifetime. Such a portrait does not survive now, but it (or a copy of it) might have been known to the carvers of the Heads. Strikingly, too, the Head is dressed in a fashionable style appropriate to the early 1400s and, taken with its pose and demeanour, the identification as James I is probably secure. Also present are James V's two wives, Madeleine de Valois and Mary of Guise. Several of these 'family' Heads are surrounded by honorific ostrich plumes and some of the borders also share similar styles.

Above: Replica Head 12, representing James V.

IDENTIFYING A NOBLE PAGAN

Head 7 has been identified as Julius Caesar from its close resemblance to a figure in *The Three Good Pagans*, an early 16th-century print by the German artist Hans Burgkmair. As a great leader, Julius Caesar was one of the Famous Men of the historic past and also one of the Nine Worthies. He might have been included in either capacity or both.

Such figures raise fascinating speculations about how subjects were chosen for the Heads and where the designs were located. One figure who must have been present in the original scheme was Godefroy de Bouillon, the crusader who was one of the Nine Worthies and considered to be an ancestor of Mary of Guise. But none of the surviving Heads can be related to any of the known images of this prestigious figure.

Above: Hans Burgkmair's engraving, *The Three Good Pagans*, depicting Hector, Alexander and Julius Caesar.

Above: Head 7, identified as Julius Caesar from the spiked crown in Burgkmair's engraving.

CONTEMPORARY FIGURES

Another group represents James's contemporaries and more extended family, people such as the Holy Roman Emperor Charles V (one of the finest of the Heads and surely based on a good portrait) and James's uncle, Henry VIII of England. Henry VIII has been identified not just by his general appearance and the (English) lion draped over his shoulders but by his full-face image, staring straight out at us, a pose unique among the Heads and rare in contemporary portraiture – except for depictions of Henry.

Dynasty was an important idea in the 1500s. Scots historians of the early part of the century often give extended royal family trees stretching far back into the mythic past. A king whose ancestors had been kings for centuries was, in many eyes, more kingly than one whose family had only recently gained royal authority. And such claims might be supported by the display of fantastical family trees and of 'portraits' of remote 'ancestors'. In similar vein, one of the external statues has been tentatively identified as King Fergus, a semi-mythical ancient king said to have introduced law into Scotland.

Since kings, queens and courts are inextricably associated with courtiers, there are several of those as well. A striking example is the poet, in classic 'hand on heart' pose, while another is a woman in a masquing costume, a disguise worn for courtly entertainments. A third (Head 24) wears a chain of office and might be John, 4th Duke of Albany, kinsman of the king and regent of Scotland during part of his childhood. The two *putti* (cherubs) and the jester can be seen as part of this group, too.

Above: Replica Head 39, showing Henry VIII of England, before it was painted.

Above: Original Head 13, showing the Holy Roman Emperor Charles V.

FAMOUS MEN OF THE PAST

The largest single group comprises Famous Men of the past, men understood by humanist scholars of the 1500s to display exemplary moral behaviour. Most prominent of these are the four representations of Hercules, who chose a life of struggle and virtue to perform his famous labours and was to be rewarded with immortality (see page 160–1). Also in this group are six Roman emperors, four wearing armour, though, as was usual at this time, the armour is rather fanciful.

Closely related to the Famous Men were the Nine Worthies. Representatives of an older, medieval and chivalric ideal of leadership, they comprise three Jewish, three pre-Christian and three Christian men. A Head of Julius Caesar, based on a print by Hans Burgkmair, would qualify as an emperor but he was also one of the Nine Worthies. Some of the Nine Female Worthies may also be present, though they cannot be personally identified.

Decorative schemes incorporating Famous Men and Worthies in various media were quite widespread at this time, but usually in public spaces where their exemplary lessons were best appreciated. Their relevance in Scotland is vividly shown by Robert Wedderburn in his 1559 essay 'The Complaynt of Scotland'. In it, he underlines Mary of Guise's descent from Godefroy de Bouillon, one of the three Christian Worthies. De Bouillon was the paragon of crusader knights, whose feat in shooting three birds with one arrow is commemorated in Mary's coat of arms. Even more directly, Wedderburn compares her with such Female Worthies as Lucretia, Penelope and Penthesilea (Queen of the Amazons) as a clever and bold leader of her (adoptive) nation. Much earlier, around 1375, the poet John Barbour had compared Robert the Bruce to Judas Maccabaeus, one of the three Jewish Worthies.

Above: The original Head 33, which shows Hercules killing the Nemean Lion.

Right: A Greek marble sculpture of Hercules and the Nemean Lion, dating from the 4th century BC.

So, the intention was that important visitors would see the king, sitting below this ceiling, presented in the context of his court, his ancestors and his European contemporaries and accompanied by exemplary figures of the heroic, historic and chivalric past. The company he keeps could be interpreted as evidence of his own merits; while his long royal ancestry and eminent extended family are evidence of his right to rule, adding to his prestige as a Christian and noble king. The presence of his mother and her brother Henry VIII emphasise, also, his potential claim to the throne of England. His image was there, on permanent display, even when the real king was absent. And it was in a setting of astonishing modernity. The visual impact which the ceiling has on modern visitors, even at first glance, is obvious. With the addition of these more complex messages, the impact must have been greatly increased – certainly more than enough to explain why the king commissioned the work, though of course he may never have lived to see the full effect.

WHO CARVED THE HEADS?

Three likely carvers are named in the contemporary documents, with one or more masters working with a small team, including apprentices. There is great variability in the skill of the carving of the Heads as a group, and even within individual Heads. There are, however, striking similarities of detail between the Heads and the external statuary – the eyebrows of James V on the outside are very similar to those on some of the Heads, for example, and there are probably more profound links between the interior and exterior works to be researched in the future. Even more tantalising is the fact that each Head may well have been labelled with the identity painted on a ribbon on the background, and now lost forever. But if aspects of the Heads remain frustratingly mysterious, we can console ourselves that we may be sharing some of our puzzlement with the educated 16th-century visitor and, in that sense, the Heads are still performing one of their original tasks.

Above: A detail of James V's statue on the Palace exterior.

Above: The original Head 2, also depicted with heavy eyebrows, suggesting that it may be the work of the same carver.

Above: Mary of Guise's coat of arms, as depicted in stained glass at the Palace. At its centre are three birds – a reference to her ancestor Godefroy de Bouillon.

REPLICA HEADS: JOHN DONALDSON

Above: John Donaldson at work on replica Head 20.

John Donaldson knows the Stirling Heads better than anyone except for the original carvers. He lived with them for five years and even now he says, 'I am still altering my views on why things were done as they were.' It is this open-mindedness that has made John a key member of the research team, as well as being the carver commissioned to create the new Heads. 'By nature, I'm curious,' he says. 'When I was a child on the beach I wondered what I was going to find under the next stone. So this was a perfect job for me.'

Aspects of the work perplex him. Why was the carving so deep if the resulting sense of drama was going to be obscured by painting? Three of the cherubs on Head 13 (Charles V) are superbly carved. 'But the one on the left has an asymmetrical face and an ear where the others have none; and the whole performance is lumpen.' He is certain that this sort of variation, with 'apprentice mistakes' next to first-rate artistry, must relate to the way the work was organised.

Perhaps John's most striking discovery was the realisation that, on the border of one carving, a Female Worthy (Head 20), the pattern of 0s, Is and IIs could be meaningful, and, after long puzzling, he identified this as medieval musical notation. It's the sort of insight which could only come from deep immersion in the detail of the Heads – what John calls 'experiential archaeology'.

His excitement about the project is obvious but one Head gives him particular pleasure. There were 36 Heads to be copied, but space for 37. It was straightforward enough to design a border based on fragments from Heads which no longer exist. The dress of one of the female figures on the outside of the Palace was adapted. But what about a face? John holds up the completed Head beside his own face. Two pairs of eyes look out – and nobody could miss the resemblance between the craggy-featured man and the younger woman. 'In past centuries,' says John, 'carvers and artists would always put something of themselves into their work. And this was my opportunity. My carving style and my daughter's portrait.'

But, for all his intimate knowledge of the Heads, John is sure they still have more to tell us. 'People need to keep throwing out new ideas – some will be daft and some are worth thinking about but will then be rejected. We all make mistakes,' he says. 'Let's keep thinking about them and be open to new suggestions. Then we will keep learning about them.'

Above left: John Donaldson with his daughter Fiona, the model for Head 41.

Above right: A detail of Head 20 in production.

ROYALTY

As well as James and Mary, and both of James's parents, several other royal figures are represented among the Stirling Heads. They include both Scottish and foreign royalty, both living and dead. They signify James's dynastic right to rule and his prestigious alliances.

Above (left to right): Replica Heads 9 (James I), 13 (Charles V) and 26 (Madeleine de Valois).

Opposite: Painting replica Head 17 (Margaret Tudor). All the Heads were painted *after* being attached to the ceiling.

Opposite and above: Replica Head 39 (Henry VIII)
before and after painting.

COURT AND PAGEANTRY

One purpose of the Stirling Heads was to celebrate the
richness and sophistication of the Scottish court. These Heads
are thought to be portraits of individual courtiers, dressed in
the fashionable Continental styles of the day.

Above: A *putto* or cherub on the breast of replica Head 20.

Above (clockwise from top left): Replica Heads 16 (noblewoman in French hood), 38 (*putto*), 18 (noblewoman in Italian head-dress) and 25 (noblewoman in Italian costume and head-dress).

Above: Replica Head 28 (noblewoman in French-style *bongrace* head-dress).

Above: Replica Head 29 (woman in masquing costume).

Above: Replica Head 22 (nobleman in slashed doublet).

Above: Replica Head 23 (nobleman in slashed doublet).

Above: Replica Head 24 (thought to represent
John Stewart, 2nd Duke of Albany).

Above: Replica Head 14 (thought to represent a poet,
reciting his verses with one hand clasped to his breast).

THE NINE WORTHIES (MALE)

The Nine Worthies were a group of historical, mythical
and biblical leaders who in Renaissance times were seen as
shining examples of virtue and nobility. Several of the Heads
have been identified as Worthies. Others may have been
portrayed in Heads that have since been lost.

Above: Replica Head 1 (Worthy wearing animal-like helmet,
tentatively identified as Godefroy de Bouillon, crusader and
ancestor of Mary of Guise).

Above: Replica Head 2 (Worthy wearing battle armour, possibly
either Charlemagne or King Arthur, who was traditionally believed
to have links with Stirling).

Above: Replica Head 3 (Worthy with exotic hair and beard, which may identify him as one of the Jewish Worthies, Joshua, David and Judas Maccabeus).

Above: Replica Head 4 (Worthy wearing battle armour).

THE NINE WORTHIES (FEMALE)

As well as the male Worthies, there were also female Worthies.
One has been tentatively identified among the original
Stirling Heads, though we cannot be sure who she is, and
there may well have been others. Replica Head number 41
represents a female Worthy, using the carver's daughter as a
model, with clothing based on one of the exterior sculptures.

Above: Replica Head 20 (Female Worthy,
with musical notation in border).

Above: Replica Head 41 (Female Worthy,
modelled on carver's daughter).

Opposite: Replica Head 20 before it was painted.

ROMAN EMPERORS

For James V and his contemporaries, Classical Rome was
a pinnacle of culture, and its emperors represented military
prowess and political shrewdness. Several Roman emperors
are portrayed among the Heads. One has been identified
as Julius Caesar (see page 138) who was also one of the
Nine Worthies.

Above: Replica Head 8 (Emperor Titus).

Above: Replica Head 32 (Roman emperor, likely to be one of the
'good' emperors of the 2nd century AD, such as Antoninus Pius
and Marcus Aurelius).

Above: Replica Head 31 (Roman emperor, likely to be one of the 'good' emperors of the 2nd century AD, such as Antoninus Pius and Marcus Aurelius).

Above: Replica Head 6 (Unidentified Roman emperor, possibly Trajan).

HERCULES

Hercules was a hero of Classical mythology, the son of the god Jupiter. His greatest achievement was completing the Twelve Labours – a series of almost impossible tasks – for which he was rewarded with immortality. For James and his court, Hercules was a paragon of Classical nobility.

Above: Replica Head 5 (Hercules, with two snakes in border).

Above: Replica Head 33 (Hercules slays the Nemean Lion).

Above: Replica Head 34 (Hercules with his club).

EPILOGUE

This book has looked back over the Palace Project, reviewing the changes seen at the Palace over the last few centuries, and setting out the rationale for the re-presentation. Reopening the revitalised Palace to the public is, however, both a time for reflection and an opportunity to look to the future.

The stunning interiors, created by superb craftsmen and women, will be seen by far more people than the originals of the 1540s. And the useful life of the interiors will be longer, too, extended by modern care and conservation methods.

We now know much more about the courts of James V and of Mary of Guise, and about the extraordinary new ideas concerning the arts, philosophy and kingship that were embodied in the creation of the Palace building.

This allows the distinctive contribution to Scottish history made by James and Mary to emerge from the shadow of their famous daughter, Mary Queen of Scots.

These advances will provide stepping stones for further work, enabling historians to ask new questions. In that sense, completion of this phase of the project is also a beginning. It is an apt moment to recall the statue on the north façade of Saturn, or Old Father Time, who forever destroys but is forever new.

FURTHER READING

A. S. Cavallo, *The Unicorn Tapestries at the Metropolitan Museum of Art* (1998)

M. Chatenet, *La Cour de France au XVIe Siècle* (2002)

J. Dunbar, *The Stirling Heads*, 2nd edition (1975)

J. Dunbar, *Scottish Royal Palaces: The Architecture of the Royal Residences during the Late Medieval and Early Renaissance Periods* (1999)

R. Fawcett, *Stirling Castle* (1995)

C. McKean, *Stirling and the Trossachs* (RIAS guide) (1985)

C. Penney and J. Oxley, *The Stirling Palace Tapestries* (2009)

RCAHMS, *Inventory of Stirlingshire* (1963)

C. Tabraham, *Scotland's Castles* (2005)

A. Thomas, *Princelie Majestie: The Court of James V of Scotland, 1528–1542* (2005)

S. Thurley, *The Royal Palaces of Tudor England* (1993)

M. Vale, *The Princely Court: Medieval Courts and Culture in North-West Europe* (2001)

P. Yeoman, *Stirling Castle: Official Souvenir Guide* (2011)

CREDITS

Editor: Andrew Burnet
Consulting editor: Peter Yeoman
Design: Contagious UK Ltd

ILLUSTRATION CREDITS

Principal photography: David Henrie and Michael Brooks
Illustration, p.15: David Simon
Illustration, p.18: Jonathan Foyle
Illustrations, p.23 and p.67: David Lawrence
Illustration, p.34: Historic Scotland / Kirkdale Archaeology
Illustration, p.51: Mark D. Dennis
Illustrations, pp.96–7: Robert Nelmes
Digital image, pp.58–9: Digital Design Studio

All images © Crown copyright, reproduced courtesy of Historic Scotland except: **p.14 r:**
Ms 65 / 1284 f.1v January: Banquet Scene, from the Très Riches Heures du Duc de Berry by
Limbourg Brothers (fl.1400–16) Musée Condé / Giraudon / Bridgeman Art Library; **p.15 t:**
Netherlandish School, Portrait of a Man, called James IV, National Gallery of Scotland; **p.16 l:**
© 2011. White Images / Scala, Florence; **p.16 c:** Reproduced by kind permission of the National Trust
for Scotland; **p.16 r:** Reproduced by permission of the Trustees of the National Library of Scotland;
p.17: A Kitchen by Campi, Vincenzo (1536–91) (school of) Pinacoteca di Brera, Milan / Alinari /
Bridgeman Art Library; **p.22 tc and p.88:** © Philip Mould Ltd; **p.22 tr:** Henry VIII in his Privy Chamber
by Holbein the Younger, Hans (1497–1543) Private Collection / Bridgeman Art Library; **p.24 tl:**
© Lennoxlove House Ltd. Licensor www.scran.ac.uk; **p.24 tc:** © Bibliothèque nationale de France;
p.25 t: Portrait of Mary Stuart, Queen of Scotland (1542–87) at the age of Nine, July 1552 by Clouet
(studio of), Musée Condé / Giraudon / Bridgeman Art Library; **p.25 bl and bc:** © National Portrait
Gallery, London; **p.25 br:** Portrait of Francis II (1544–60) as Dauphin of France at the age of Eight,
1552 by Clouet (studio of), Museé Condé / Bridgeman Art Library; **p.29 tl:** Reproduced by
permission of the Trustees of the National Library of Scotland; **p.29 b:** With kind permission of The
Argyll and Sutherland Highlanders Museum Trust; **p.36 tl:** The collection at Blair Castle, Perthshire;
p.43 b: The Field of the Cloth of Gold, c.1545 by English School, The Royal Collection © 2011 Her
Majesty Queen Elizabeth II / Bridgeman Art Library; **p.45 tl and tr:** Albertina, Vienna; **p.63 bl and p.66:**
© Victoria and Albert Museum, London; **p.68:** © The British Library Board (Royal 2 A. XVI, f.3); **p.70 bl
and bc:** © Stirling Smith Art Gallery and Museum. Licensor www.scran.ac.uk; **p.70 br:** © The Trustees
of The National Museums Scotland; **p.74 tl:** © University of Strathclyde. Licensor www.scran.ac.uk;
p.77: Fresco at Malpaga Castle, Bergamo, Italy (www.castellomalpaga.it); **p.80 br:** © John Crook;
p.82: The Royal Collection © 2011, Her Majesty Queen Elizabeth II; **p.85 l:** Portrait presumed to be
Gabrielle de Rochechouart (1530–80) c.1548 by Corneille de Lyon (attr. to) Musée Condé / Giraudon /
Bridgeman Art Library; **p.85 r:** © 2011. Photo Scala, Florence – courtesy of the Ministero Beni e Att.
Culturali; **pp.86–7 and p.107 tr:** © Erich Lessing; **p.89 t:** In the collection of the Stirlings of Keir; **p.89
bc and br:** © National Museums Scotland. Licensor www.scran.ac.uk; **p.91, p.107 br, p.108 tr and
pp.115–21:** © 2011. Images copyright The Metropolitan Museum of Art / Art Resource / Scala,
Florence; **p.92:** Edward VI, c.1550 by Scrots, Guillaume (fl.1537–53) (attr. to) The Royal Collection
© 2011 Her Majesty Queen Elizabeth II / Bridgeman Art Library; **p.93:** Jane Seymour, 1536 by Holbein
the Younger, Hans, Kunsthistorisches Museum, Vienna, Austria / Bridgeman Art Library; **p.107 tl:**
The Annunciation, Brussels Workshop, c.1510 by Flemish School, St Sauveur Cathedral, Aix-en-
Provence / Giraudon / Bridgeman Art Library; **p.107 bl:** Flip Nicklin / Minden Pictures / FLPA; **p.111 t:**
© NTPL; **p.135 br:** © Wawel Royal Castle, Cracow; **p.136 bl:** Unknown, James I, Scottish National
Portrait Gallery; **p.138 l:** © The Trustees of the British Museum; **p.140 br:** Heracles fighting the
Nemean Lion, 4th century BC by Greek School, Hermitage, St Petersburg / Bridgeman Art Library.

(**t** = top; **b** = bottom; **l** = left; **r** = right; **c** = centre)

ACKNOWLEDGEMENTS

We are grateful to the following, whose advice, expertise and encouragement has
been indispensible in producing this book.

Graciela Ainsworth (*Sculpture Conservation and Restoration*)
Liz Boulton (*Embroiderers' Guild*)
Lindsay Bowditch (*Studioarc*)
Peter Buchanan (*Historic Scotland*)
Claudia Cividini (*Castello Malpaga, Bergamo, Italy*)
Owen Davison (*The Conservation Studio*)
John Donaldson (*Carver and sculptor*)
Gordon Ewart (*Kirkdale Archaeology*)
Prof Richard Fawcett (*University of St Andrews*)
Dennis Gallagher (*Kirkdale Archaeology*)
Christa Gerdwilker (*Historic Scotland*)
Bob Holsman (*Anna Visscher Ltd*)
Hilary Holsman (*Anna Visscher Ltd*)
Prof Malcolm Lochhead (*Glasgow Caledonian University*)
David Mitchell (*Historic Scotland*)
John Nevin (*MacKay Decorators*)
Michael Pearce (*Historic Scotland*)
Carron Penney (*West Dean Tapestry Studio*)
Ken Peterkin (*ArtLus Period Interiors*)
Dr Sally Rush (*University of Glasgow*)
Peter Russell (*Stuart Interiors*)
Romilly Squire (*Heraldic Artist*)
Vivienne Swatridge (*Stuart Interiors*)

This book has drawn on extensive research by members of the Stirling Palace Academic
Research Committee (SPARC). That work was co-ordinated by Historic Scotland staff,
particularly Doreen Grove, Peter Yeoman and Peter Buchanan. Dr Sally Rush and
Prof Michael Bath were key members of SPARC, generating new analytical material
and the proposals on which the internal decoration of the Palace is based. The results
of archaeological and historical research by a team from Kirkdale Archaeology
(particularly Gordon Ewart, Dennis Gallagher and John Harrison) are available at
http://sparc.scran.ac.uk/home/

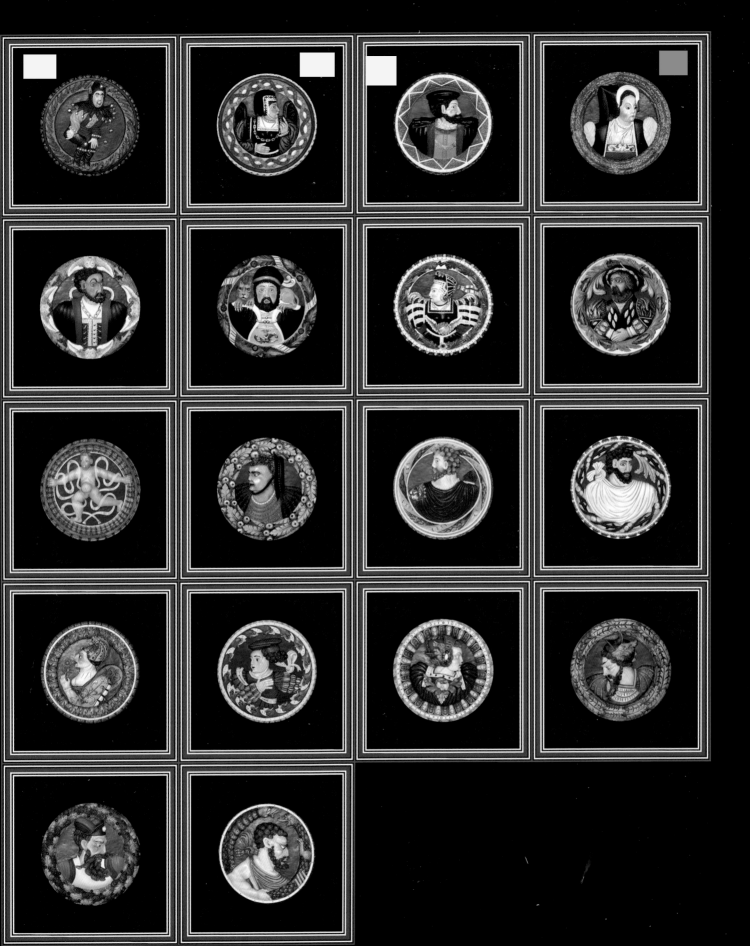